W9-BMN-838

$5.00

# PASTA FOR ALL
# SEASONS

OTHER BOOKS BY ROBIN ROBERTSON

*Rice & Spice*

*The Sacred Kitchen* (with Jon Robertson)

*The Vegetarian Chili Cookbook*

*Some Like It Hot*

*The Soy Gourmet*

*366 Simply Delicious Dairy-Free Recipes*

*366 Healthful Ways to Cook Tofu and Other Meat Alternatives*

# PASTA FOR ALL SEASONS

125 *Vegetarian Pasta*

*Recipes for*

*Family and Friends*

ROBIN ROBERTSON

*Illustrations by Melanie Marder Parks*

The Harvard Common Press
Boston, Massachusetts

## DEDICATION

This book is dedicated to the memory of my grandmother,
Lucia Pecora Gennaro

The Harvard Common Press
535 Albany Street
Boston, Massachusetts 02118

www.harvardcommonpress.com

Copyright © 2000 by Robin Robertson
Illustrations copyright © 2000 by Melanie Marder Parks

All rights reserved. No part of this publication may be reproduced or transmitted in any form or by any means, electronic or mechanical, including photocopying, recording, or any information storage or retrieval system, without permission in writing from the publisher.

Printed in the United States of America
Printed on acid-free paper

Library of Congress Cataloging-in-Publication Data

Robertson, Robin (Robin G.)
    Pasta for all seasons : 125 vegetarian pasta recipes for family and friends / Robin Robertson; illustrations by Melanie Parks.
    p. cm.
    Includes index.
    ISBN 1-55832-174-8 (hard : alk. paper) -- ISBN 1-55832-175-6 (paper : alk. paper)
        1. Vegetarian cookery. 2. Cookery (Pasta) I. Title.

TX837.R62497 2000
641.8'22--dc21
                                                    00-039626

Special bulk-order discounts are available on this and other Harvard Common Press books. Companies and organizations may purchase books for premiums or for resale, or may arrange a custom edition, by contacting the Marketing Director at the address above.

Cover photograph by Envision
Cover design by Suzanne Noli
Text design by Kay Schuckhart/Blond on Pond
Illustrations by Melanie Marder Parks

10 9 8 7 6 5 4 3 2 1

# ACKNOWLEDGMENTS

I'd like to acknowledge my family, friends, and colleagues for their help during the writing of this book. Special thanks to my husband and favorite pasta partner, Jon, for his unwavering enthusiasm while sampling numerous pasta creations and also for his talented technical support; to Gloria Seigel for her diligent testing—and her husband, Mel, for his diligent tasting; to B.J. Atkinson for testing recipes and sharing her soup recipe; and to Samantha Ragan, Lochlain Lewis, Pat Davis, and John Mein for their support and encouragement. Thanks, also, to Dan Rosenberg and the staff at The Harvard Common Press for helping to make this book a reality.

# CONTENTS

# INTRODUCTION

Over the last three decades, a quiet pasta revolution has taken place. American pasta meals have evolved from an occasional spaghetti dinner to a virtual pasta obsession. Not long ago, only a few lonely brands of spaghetti nestled between the elbow macaroni and egg noodles on the grocer's shelf, but these days, we can enjoy literally hundreds of different pasta and sauce combinations any time the mood strikes. Supermarket shelves are now lined with dozens of pasta shapes, flavors, and varieties. Restaurant chefs employ pasta as a blank canvas for imaginative menu creations as home cooks rely on pasta to provide quick, easy, and economical dinners.

Back in the days when pasta was popularly known as spaghetti or macaroni, I was fortunate to have grown up with what could be called "pasta consciousness." My awareness of pasta's importance in the grand culinary scheme stemmed from the fact that my Italian-American family couldn't get enough. Twice-weekly pasta meals were standard, although three times per week was not uncommon. During the week, pasta was served "American style"—as an entree rather than a first course as they do in Italy. On Thursdays, we often feasted on linguine, ziti, or my favorite, perciatelli—liberally ladled with my mother's rich tomato sauce. At least twice a month, a Friday night supper featured *pasta fagiole,* the hearty pasta and bean soup. Sunday was reserved for homemade specialties such as ravioli, cavatelli, or gnocchi, which were served as a separate course, in the classic Italian manner.

Later in life I was surprised to meet people whose only pasta experience had been spaghetti with a canned sauce or macaroni and cheese out of a box. These days, however, as global cuisines become part of our everyday fare, the glorious strands and shapes of Italian pastas are familiar to nearly everyone who enjoys food.

It's no wonder people love pasta—it's perfect anytime. It's easy to cook, economical, nutritious, convenient, and it tastes great. Pasta is enjoyed equally by finicky children, cash-strapped students, health-conscious athletes, and discerning gourmands.

What other food is so versatile that one could literally eat it any day of the year and not get bored?

Pasta comes in all sizes, from the tiny acini de pepe (peppercorn-shaped pasta) that is used in soups to the large conchiglie (shells) for stuffing. Many types of pasta are given poetic names that describe their shapes such as mostaccioli (little mustaches) and farfalle (butterflies or bow ties). Strand pastas include the delicate capellini or angel hair, and the ubiquitous spaghetti, linguine, and fettuccine.

Most traditional Italian pasta is made from enriched semolina flour ground from hard durum wheat. For those who are wheat-sensitive, natural foods stores carry pastas made from quinoa, corn, spelt, and rice. Pasta can also vary in color and taste. A variety of herbs, vegetables, and seasonings can be added to pasta dough to produce artichoke, tomato, and spinach pastas, or more exotic varieties flavored with ingredients such as wild mushrooms, beets, and chiles. Dried pasta is the most common and inexpensive type and offers the most variety of shapes. Fresh pasta is more costly and usually available commercially only in strands or sheets. Several high-quality brands of both dried and fresh pasta can be found in well-stocked supermarkets and specialty food shops.

Adding to the variety of the pastas is the seemingly limitless range of toppings. Most classic pasta sauces are based on tomato, olive oil, or cream, depending on the Italian region of origin. However, these days one is liable to find pasta combined with virtually any ingredients imaginable. Pasta sauces can be as simple and quick as a drizzle of olive oil to a rich, long-simmered creation made with exotic ingredients.

## A PASTA PRIMER

The origin of pasta can be traced to a number of sources. Pasta-making is said to be depicted on the wall of a fourth-century B.C. Etruscan tomb. One legend credits the Greek god Vulcan with creating an invention that made strings of dough. Some say pasta was introduced to Italy by Marco Polo upon his return from the Far East, where Chinese history traces noodle-making to 3000 B.C. Still another source names Arabia as pasta's place of origin.

While the Chinese or Arabians may have invented the noodle, it was the Italians who created the poetry of pasta. Where else is one simple food fashioned in such incredible variety? Each shape and strand has been christened lovingly with playfully evocative names. To this day, pasta is synonymous with Italy, where it is eaten enthusiastically every day, although it is fast becoming an all-American favorite as well.

Ever since Thomas Jefferson first introduced "macaroni" to the New World, pasta has been a presence on American dinner tables. The last quarter of the twentieth century saw a virtual pasta renaissance, with one survey reporting that 77 percent of Americans eat pasta at least once a week.

## Fresh or Dried?

Pasta can be purchased fresh or dried, each having its unique taste and texture. Dried pasta, made with semolina flour from durum wheat, is the kind of pasta you find in boxes on supermarket shelves. These pastas boast a wide variety of shapes and are economical and convenient. Dried pasta is made commercially by an extrusion process.

Fresh pasta, on the other hand, is usually made with all-purpose flour and eggs, and the soft dough is rolled through a hand-cranked or electric pasta machine. Pasta machines are available for home use and pasta can be fun and satisfying to make at home, especially when compared with the price of fresh pasta from specialty food shops. Still, to many people, time is their most valued resource, and with fresh pasta readily available in supermarkets and specialty shops, many fresh pasta enthusiasts are purchasing their product rather than making it themselves.

Both dried and fresh pasta can produce delicious results, so the choice is largely a matter of personal taste. Many people, including the southern Italians, prefer the chewy texture of dried pasta over the tender doughiness of fresh, which is favored in the north.

## Cooking Pasta

Dried pasta takes longer to cook than fresh, usually three to fifteen minutes, depending on the shape and quality of the pasta. The preferred cooked texture is slightly firm, called *al dente* or "firm to the bite." Fresh pasta cooks in one to three minutes, producing more tender results. The basic cooking method for pasta is to cook it in a large amount of salted, rapidly boiling water (a minimum of four to five quarts per pound) until done. To save time, be sure to add the salt *after* the water comes to a boil, since unsalted water boils faster. Also keep a lid on your pot when bringing the water to a boil. Once the pasta is added to the pot, cook uncovered, stirring frequently. Pasta cooking times are measured beginning when the water returns to a boil after the pasta has been added.

Test for doneness by retrieving a piece of pasta from the water and biting into it. Since it is important not to overcook pasta, it is best not to rely solely on the cooking time recommended on the box or in the recipes, but to begin testing a few minutes beforehand to ensure that it is done to your liking. For a pasta that is supposed to be cooked in ten minutes, for example, start testing it for doneness after about eight minutes.

Be sure to stir the pasta several times during the cooking process to prevent pieces from sticking to the bottom of the pot and to each other. Pasta should be drained well in a colander before adding sauces or other ingredients.

Cooked pasta should be rinsed after draining only when it is used in pasta salads or other cold dishes, or if it will not be used immediately. In such instances, pasta should be rinsed under cold water to stop the cooking process and then be drained well. Otherwise, it is important *not* to rinse pasta because it makes it difficult for the sauce to adhere and may wash away some of the nutrients.

One pound of uncooked pasta will produce up to eight cups cooked. Most of the recipes in this book call for one pound of pasta to yield four main-course servings. As a first course, one pound of pasta would serve six to eight people, depending on the dish.

Dried pasta should be stored sealed, in a cool dry place, where it will keep for up to a year. For best retention of nutrients, dried pasta should not be exposed to light. Fresh pasta keeps well refrigerated for several days or frozen for up to a month.

## Pasta Shapes

In addition to the flat and round strands and extruded Italian pasta shapes, there are also a number of pasta types that are meant specifically for stuffing and layering such as cannelloni, manicotti, lasagna, and large shells. There are too many shapes and sizes to list them all (estimates range from 300 to 700, depending on the source), however, here are some of the more common varieties:

♦ Round strands: angel hair or capellini, vermicelli, spaghettini, spaghetti, perciatelli

- Flat ribbons: linguine, fettuccine, pappardelle, tagliatelle, lasagna

- Small shapes: acini di pepe, ditalini, orzo, stellini

- Tubular shapes: penne, ziti, rigatoni, mostaccioli

- Curved shapes: farfalle, orecchiette, radiatore, conchiglie, ruote, elbows

- Curly shapes: fusilli, gemelli, cavatappi, rotelle, rotini

- Stuffed pasta: tortellini, ravioli, agnolotti

- Shapes for stuffing: large shells, manicotti, cannelloni

- Others: there are specialty and seasonal shapes such as red and green pasta Christmas trees, as well as a wide variety of flavored pastas

## SAUCING THE PASTA

Tradition dictates, and many food experts agree, that particular pasta shapes should be paired with certain types of sauces. Often the thinner pastas are teamed with the lighter olive oil and creamy sauces, while the thicker, sturdier pastas stand up to the heavier, more robust toppings. Certain classic pasta and sauce combinations such as fettuccine Alfredo, linguine alla pesto, and penne arrabbiata have become the inseparable pairs of the pasta world.

Increasingly, however, the lines cross and the same pasta shape may be tossed with olive oil and fresh herbs, topped with a hearty puttanesca sauce, or found floating in a delicate broth.

To my thinking, some rules were made to be broken. While I do pay homage to many pasta and sauce classics, I also enjoy the many surprises I've found while teaming unconventional partners. The recipes in this book reflect what I've found to be memorable pasta and sauce combinations, some traditional, some not. In each case, you are encouraged to try my suggestion but at the same time to use your own creativity and imagination to come up with your own favorite combinations. To me, part of the pleasure of pasta is experimenting with different shape and sauce combinations. At the end of each recipe, alternate pasta suggestions are given in case the one listed in the recipe is unavailable. If you wish to try a particular recipe that calls for a pasta type you do not have on hand, your own creative combination may prove to be the best recipe yet.

Pasta shapes such as manicotti, large shells, lasagna, or ravioli can be stuffed with a variety of flavorful fillings that often include ricotta cheese or tofu. Baked pasta dishes such as lasagne are extremely versatile and well suited to feeding a crowd. They can be cloaked in a red or white sauce and may include a number of vegetables for delicious variations. Another popular baked pasta dish is macaroni and cheese, a familiar comfort food. And don't forget the versatile and party-friendly pasta salad. The growing interest in ethnic cuisines has given rise to the popularity of Asian noodle dishes such as China's lo mein, Thailand's pad thai, and Japan's yaki soba. While traditional Asian noodles are generally used to make these dishes, I've found that Italian pastas such as vermicelli, linguine, and fettuccine produce excellent results as well.

## THE PASTA PANTRY

Few foods are easier to cook than pasta—it's literally as easy as boiling water. While the water comes to a boil, you can assemble the sauce ingredients and dinner can often be ready by the time the pasta is cooked. Most of the recipes in this book can be prepared in thirty minutes or less.

Pasta can be used to enrich soups such as minestrone or made into a versatile pasta salad. Noodles are also used as a bed for goulash and other stews, or baked in casseroles such as macaroni and cheese. While the most familiar pasta dishes hail from Italy, Asian noodle dishes are fast becoming popular mainstays as well. However, it is not absolutely necessary to purchase these specialty noodles to enjoy the great flavors of Asia, as the recipes included in this book demonstrate.

If you keep several kinds of pasta on hand, along with a variety of sauce ingredients, you'll never again be stumped at dinnertime. Stock your pantry with prepared sauces, extra-virgin olive oil, and a variety of canned tomato products, including paste, puree, and diced and whole tomatoes. Dried or canned bean varieties should include chickpeas, cannellini beans, lentils, kidney beans, favas, and borlotti beans, if you can find them.

Line your shelves with sun-dried tomatoes, artichoke hearts, olives, dried mushrooms, capers, and roasted red peppers. Always keep a supply of fresh garlic, onions, and shallots on hand—they store well and can be the starting point for many fabulous dishes. For those times when you want pasta with an Asian flair, be sure to include tamari sauce, sesame oil, chili paste, and other Asian flavor-enhancers in your pasta pantry.

By keeping an arsenal of pasta and complementary ingredients on hand, you'll always be ready to create a variety of nourishing and flavorful meals in minutes.

## PASTA: A HEALTH FOOD?

When it comes to health foods, pasta may not be the first thing that comes to mind. After all, many pasta dishes are smothered in rich sauces made with heavy cream, cheeses, and meats. These days, however, pasta is more likely to be updated with fresh light sauces that include more vegetables and less meat and dairy products. While pasta purists may consider an Alfredo sauce made with tofu heretical, a growing number of people are looking for lighter ways to enjoy their favorite dishes.

Pasta is an important part of a well-balanced diet. Many people are looking for ways to include more grains in their diet since the USDA Food Guide Pyramid recommends we eat six to eleven (one-half cup) servings of complex carbohydrates per day. A steaming bowl of your favorite pasta is a delicious way to help meet that recommendation. In addition to being low in fat and sodium, commercially produced pasta is enriched with iron, B vitamins, and other nutrients.

Vegetarians and other health-conscious people rely on the high energy and nutrition they can get from a pasta meal, especially when combined with vegetables, beans, and other ingredients such as soy products. Although many classic pasta sauces include cheese, heavy cream, butter, and meat, it is easy to make satisfying and delicious versions of these sauces without meat or dairy products. This is good news for vegans, people watching their weight or cholesterol, and for those seeking healthier recipes that everyone can enjoy. Since many cookbooks containing vegetarian pasta recipes are still loaded with dairy products, I felt it was important to make the recipes in this book accessible to everyone—from health-conscious meat eaters, to vegetarians, to vegans. For that reason, in addition to being meatless, the recipes in this book are "dairy optional"—that is, I provide vegan options for each recipe that lists dairy as an ingredient.

The trend toward healthy eating is moving away from the use of dairy products owing to their high fat and cholesterol content, as well as concern over ingesting pesticides, antibiotics, and other additives that can be found in milk. In addition, many medical studies recommend that we eat more soy products, including the USDA, which suggests that eating 25 grams of soy protein per day can reduce the risk of heart disease. As such, more people are searching for delicious ways to enjoy tofu and other soy products. To that end, I've retooled many classic sauces that would normally contain meat or cream into meatless and dairy-free versions that taste wonderful and are good for you, too.

Despite high-protein diet fads that avoid carbohydrates, a well-balanced, plant-based diet that includes lots of grains, beans, vegetables, and fruits continues to be a wise choice for the long haul. A great-tasting pasta meal, replete with vegetables and plant proteins, is an ideal way to enjoy all these foods. With all these healthful ingredients available, is it any wonder why the so-called Mediterranean diet, rich in olive oil, fresh vegetables, and pasta, is considered one of the healthiest diets in the world?

## Say Cheese

To many people, pasta is simply not pasta without a sprinkling of good Parmesan cheese. For that reason, many of the recipes include freshly grated cheese as an ingredient, although nondairy cheese alternatives are also provided to allow for individual choice. Still, cheese lovers are encouraged to do as the Italians do: exercise discretion and discrimination when adding cheese to pasta to avoid overpowering the other flavors of the dish. Unless cheese is an integral part of the recipe, it is best to serve it separately, passing a bowl of freshly grated cheese at the table.

The most popular cheese to serve with pasta is Parmigiano-Reggiano, a hard, tangy cheese make from cow's milk, which is aged for at least two years. Vying for second place is Pecorino Romano, a hard cheese made from sheep's milk, which has a sharper, saltier flavor than Parmesan. It is best used with spicy sauces from the southern regions of Italy. Although these cheeses can be quite expensive, a little goes a long way, thanks to their rich, full-bodied flavors. If you're looking for a cheese that is slightly less costly but still full of flavor, try some Grana Padano or Asiago, hard Italian cheeses that are similar to Parmesan. To preserve its freshness, buy cheese in whole pieces and grate as needed or when ready to serve.

Soy Parmesan is available in natural foods stores for vegans, people allergic to dairy, and others who want to avoid dairy products.

## About Olive Oil

Without a doubt, olive oil is the oil of choice in Italian cooking. But it's important to pick the right one for the job. Olive oils are graded according to how they are processed and the difference lies in the pressing.

Extra-virgin olive oil is cold-pressed without chemicals or additives, resulting in the most flavorful and most costly grade. Greenish gold in color, extra-virgin olive oil has less than 1 percent acidity, and should not be subject to high temperatures, as heating it can alter its fruity, rich flavor. It is therefore most flavorful when used on salads or in recipes that don't require long or hot cooking. It can be used to make pestos and other cold pasta sauces, or drizzled on warm pasta.

With a slightly higher acidity ratio, virgin olive oil withstands heat better than extra-virgin and can be used for cooking. Since it is also cold-pressed, it has a full rich flavor, though not as intense as extra-virgin. It is also less expensive than extra-virgin.

Pure olive oil is the most common and least expensive olive oil. It is not a cold-pressed oil, but is, instead, refined by various methods including heat, bleach, and solvents. Pure olive oil lacks the rich flavor of virgin olive oils, and because of its chemical processing, I do not recommend it.

In the recipes that follow, when olive oil is listed, you can use either virgin or extra-virgin olive oil, depending on your preference. In those instances when nothing less than extra-virgin olive oil will do, it has been specified as such in the recipe.

## PASTA: FOR ALL SEASONS

*Pasta for All Seasons* is so named because its 125 recipes are packed with the rich flavors of fresh, seasonal produce and other flavorful ingredients that can be enjoyed any time of the year. The book is filled with quick and easy recipes that taste like you've spent all day in the kitchen. It contains different ways to enjoy pasta, including winter soups and summer salads. There's a chapter devoted solely to variations on the classic tomato sauce, including fresh sauces to make when summer's crop is at its peak of flavor. Another chapter is dedicated to baked and stuffed pasta dishes destined to warm a winter kitchen. Other chapters feature pasta recipes using olive oil, garlic, herbs, and a glorious selection of vegetables, as well as protein-rich beans, nuts, and soy products. Traditional cream- and cheese-laden pasta recipes are reinvented with variations using tofu and other dairy alternatives that significantly pare down the cholesterol and fat content without sacrificing flavor.

Whether you are a card-carrying pasta addict like me, or just enjoy cooking quick and easy recipes that are both delicious and healthful any day of the year, then I hope you will enjoy using *Pasta for All Seasons* as much as I enjoyed writing it.

# PASTA FOR ALL
# SEASONS

# Aglio and Olio and Pesto, Too

Olive oil and garlic can provide the beginnings of flavorful pasta dishes that are also some of the fastest recipes imaginable. Many of these sauces are so quick that it is often best to put on the pasta water first. For example, once the water boils, the classic Capellini Aglio e Olio (page 5) can be on the table within five minutes. Other sauces, such as basil pesto and its variations, require no cooking at all and actually benefit from being prepared in advance.

Made with full-bodied olive oil and redolent of garlic, fresh herbs, and other flavorful ingredients, these recipes are bound to become household favorites—the ones you'll rely on to serve with fresh pasta, capellini, vermicelli, or other quick-cooking pasta when time is of the essence.

Capellini Aglio e Olio

Rigatoni with Olive Oil and Hot Red Pepper Flakes

Fettuccine with Garlic and Sun-Dried Tomatoes

Farfalle with Golden Raisins and Caramelized Shallots

Fusilli with Garlic, Figs, and Rosemary

Perciatelli with Garlicky Mushroom Sauce

Lemon Zest and Yellow Tomato Radiatore

Ziti with Artichoke Hearts and Kalamata Olives

Linguine and Oyster Mushrooms with Gremolata

Linguini with Basil Pesto

Ziti with Red Pepper–Walnut Pesto

Farfalle with Almond-Tarragon Pesto

Fettuccine with Cilantro-Lime Pesto

Penne with Roasted Red Pepper Pesto

Angel Hair Pasta with Parsley-Walnut Pesto

Ziti with Black Olive Tapenade

# Capellini Aglio e Olio

This dish is the essence of simplicity. Using a very thin dried pasta (or a fresh variety) takes full advantage of the quick preparation time of the sauce. In the classic dish, only olive oil, garlic, and a little salt and pepper are used, so parsley is listed as an optional garnish. Cheese is not traditionally used on many olive-oil based pasta dishes. Use full-bodied extra-virgin olive oil for the best flavor.

½ cup extra-virgin olive oil
3 large garlic cloves, finely minced
1 pound capellini
Salt and freshly ground black pepper
Minced fresh flat-leaf parsley, optional

Put a large pot of water on to boil. While waiting for the water to boil, heat ¼ cup of the olive oil in a small skillet over medium heat, add the garlic and cook, stirring until fragrant and softened, about 1 minute. Be careful not to brown the garlic. Keep warm over low heat. When the water boils, salt it, then add the capellini and cook, stirring occasionally, until it is al dente, about 2 to 4 minutes. When the pasta is cooked, drain it and place in a serving bowl. Add the garlic sauce, the remaining ¼ cup of olive oil, and salt and pepper to taste. Toss well and serve immediately, topped with parsley, if you like.

*Serves 4*

OTHER PASTA CHOICES: vermicelli, spaghettini

# Rigatoni with Olive Oil and Hot Red Pepper Flakes

A spicy variation on the classic *aglio e olio*. You can alter the amount of red pepper flakes according to personal preference. Flat-leaf parsley, which is more flavorful than the curly variety, is traditionally used in Italian cooking.

1 pound rigatoni
½ cup extra-virgin olive oil
2 large garlic cloves, finely minced
¾ teaspoon hot red pepper flakes, or to taste
2 tablespoons minced fresh flat-leaf parsley
Salt
Freshly grated Parmesan or soy Parmesan cheese

Cook the rigatoni in a large pot of salted boiling water, stirring occasionally, until it is al dente, about 8 to 10 minutes. While the pasta is cooking, heat ¼ cup of the olive oil in a small skillet over medium heat. Add the garlic and cook until soft and fragrant, about 1 minute.  Be careful not to brown the garlic. Stir in the red pepper flakes and set aside. When the pasta is cooked, drain it and place in a serving bowl. Add the garlic sauce, the remaining ¼ cup of olive oil, the parsley, and salt to taste. Toss well and serve immediately, passing a bowl of grated cheese at the table, if you like.

*Serves 4*

OTHER PASTA CHOICES: I chose the chewy rigatoni to help tone down the heat from the red pepper, but if saving time is important, use any of the thin or fresh pasta varieties.

# Fettuccine with Garlic and Sun-Dried Tomatoes

In Italy, sun-dried tomatoes are more likely to be found on an antipasto platter than as a component of a pasta dish, but I think the combination is wonderful. Fresh fettuccine may be substituted for dried, if you like. This will reduce the cooking time significantly.

1 pound fettuccine
½ cup extra-virgin olive oil
2 large garlic cloves, finely minced
½ cup sun-dried tomatoes in olive oil, drained and chopped
2 tablespoons minced fresh basil
Salt and freshly ground black pepper
Freshly grated Parmesan or soy Parmesan cheese

Cook the fettuccine in a large pot of salted boiling water, stirring occasionally, until it is al dente, about 10 minutes. While the pasta is cooking, heat ¼ cup of the olive oil in a medium skillet over medium heat. Add the garlic and cook until soft and fragrant, about 2 minutes. Be careful not to brown the garlic. Stir in the sun-dried tomatoes and set aside. When the pasta is cooked, drain it and place in a serving bowl. Add the sauce, the remaining ¼ cup of olive oil, the basil, and salt and pepper to taste. Toss well and serve immediately, topped with grated cheese, if you like.

*Serves 4*

OTHER PASTA CHOICES: linguine, spaghetti

# Farfalle with Golden Raisins and Caramelized Shallots

The sweetness of the caramelized shallots is enhanced by golden raisins in this simple but satisfying dish. Raisins are a common ingredient in Sicilian cooking, owing to the Middle Eastern influence from the seventh-century Moslem invasions.

1 pound farfalle
⅓ cup extra-virgin olive oil
1 cup shallots, quartered lengthwise
⅓ cup golden raisins
Salt and freshly ground black pepper
Minced fresh flat-leaf parsley, for garnish

Cook the farfalle in a large pot of salted boiling water, stirring occasionally, until it is al dente, about 8 to 10 minutes. While the pasta is cooking, heat 2 tablespoons of the oil in a large skillet over medium heat. Add the shallots and cook until softened, about 5 minutes. Reduce heat to low and continue cooking until the shallots are lightly browned and caramelized, about 5 to 7 minutes longer. Stir in the raisins and keep warm over low heat. When the pasta is cooked, drain it well and place in a serving bowl. Drizzle with the remaining olive oil, add the sauce, and season with salt and pepper to taste. Sprinkle with minced parsley, toss gently, and serve immediately.

*Serves 4*

OTHER PASTA CHOICES: cavatappi, gemelli

# Fusilli with Garlic, Figs, and Rosemary

This recipe was inspired by a traditional dish my family enjoyed on Christmas Eve. My mother would make homemade tagliatelle and toss it with a tasty mixture of figs, breadcrumbs, and sugar. In recent years, I've begun adding rosemary, which I think makes a fragrant addition to the dish.

½ cup olive oil
½ cup dried breadcrumbs
1 teaspoon sugar
1 tablespoon minced fresh rosemary
1 pound fusilli
2 large garlic cloves, finely minced
1 cup fresh figs, chopped
Salt and freshly ground black pepper

Heat 1 tablespoon of the oil in a small skillet over medium heat. Add the breadcrumbs and stir until lightly browned. Sprinkle on the sugar and half the rosemary, stirring to blend. Set aside. Cook the fusilli in a large pot of salted boiling water, stirring occasionally, until it is al dente, about 8 to 10 minutes. While the pasta is cooking, heat the remaining oil in a small skillet over medium heat. Add the garlic and cook until soft and fragrant, about 2 minutes. Be careful not to brown the garlic. Add the figs and the remaining rosemary, and keep warm over low heat. When the pasta is cooked, drain it and place in a serving bowl. Add the fig mixture, the breadcrumb mixture, and salt and pepper to taste. Toss well and serve immediately.

*Serves 4*

OTHER PASTA CHOICES: pappardelle, fettuccine, or perciatelli

# Perciatelli with Garlicky Mushroom Sauce

Mushrooms and garlic are a great combination and this sauce uses plenty of both. For a more pronounced flavor, you can use fresh cremini or porcini mushrooms, now widely available in supermarkets, but regular white mushrooms also produce excellent results.

> 1 pound perciatelli
> ¼ cup extra-virgin olive oil
> 4 large garlic cloves, pressed
> 8 ounces mushrooms, sliced (2½ cups)
> 1 teaspoon minced fresh or ½ teaspoon dried savory
> Salt and freshly ground black pepper
> 2 tablespoons minced fresh flat-leaf parsley

Cook the perciatelli in a large pot of salted boiling water, stirring occasionally, until it is al dente, about 10 minutes. While the pasta is cooking, heat the oil in a large skillet over medium heat, add the garlic and mushrooms, and cook, stirring until fragrant, about 1 minute. Add the savory and salt and pepper to taste, and keep warm over low heat. When the pasta is cooked, drain it and place in a serving bowl. Add the sauce and parsley, and toss well. Serve immediately.

*Serves 4*

OTHER PASTA CHOICES: I like the way thick, chewy perciatelli stands up to the earthy flavor of the sauce, but fettuccine or linguine are also fine.

# Lemon Zest and Yellow Tomato Radiatore

Radiatore, or "little radiators," are used in this light and lively pasta dish made with fresh yellow tomatoes. Miso, a concentrated soybean paste, adds a salty richness to this sauce. A traditional Japanese ingredient used to make soups and enrich sauces and dressings, miso is a blend of fermented soybeans and grains that is said to have many health benefits. It is available at natural foods stores.

1 pound radiatore
¼ cup extra-virgin olive oil
1 large garlic clove, pressed
Juice and zest of 1 lemon
2 teaspoons white miso paste
⅓ cup hot water
3 or 4 yellow tomatoes, chopped (2 to 2½ cups)
2 tablespoons snipped fresh chives
Salt and freshly ground white pepper

Cook the radiatore in a large pot of salted boiling water, stirring occasionally, until it is al dente, about 8 minutes. While the pasta is cooking, heat the oil in a large skillet over medium heat. Add the garlic and cook until fragrant, about 30 seconds. Reduce heat to very low, and stir in lemon juice and zest. Blend the miso into the hot water until smooth and stir it into the sauce. Add the tomatoes and keep warm over low heat. When the pasta is cooked, drain it and place in a serving bowl. Add the sauce, chives, salt and white pepper to taste, and toss gently to combine. Serve immediately.

*Serves 4*

OTHER PASTA CHOICES: orecchiette, rotini

# Ziti with Artichoke Hearts and Kalamata Olives

On-hand ingredients team up to create a quick and easy pasta dish that is special enough to serve to guests. The shiny black Kalamata olives from Greece are especially good in this dish, but Italian gaeta olives would be a fine substitute.

1 pound ziti
¼ cup extra-virgin olive oil
2 garlic cloves, minced
½ teaspoon hot red pepper flakes, or to taste
1 (14-ounce) can artichoke hearts, drained and quartered
½ cup pitted Kalamata olives
1 tablespoon fresh lemon juice
2 tablespoons minced fresh flat-leaf parsley
Salt and freshly ground black pepper
Freshly shaved Parmesan or soy Parmesan cheese

Cook the ziti in a large pot of salted boiling water, stirring occasionally, until it is al dente, about 8 to 10 minutes. While the pasta is cooking, heat the oil in a large skillet over medium heat. Add the garlic, red pepper flakes, artichokes, olives, lemon juice, parsley, and salt and pepper to taste, and cook until heated through, about 3 to 5 minutes. When the ziti is cooked, drain it and place in a serving bowl. Add the sauce, and toss to combine. Serve immediately, passing a bowl of cheese at the table.

*Serves 4*

OTHER PASTA CHOICES: penne or other tubular pasta

# Linguine and Oyster Mushrooms with Gremolata

Gremolata, sometimes spelled "gremolada," is a zesty mixture of garlic, lemon, and parsley that brings out the slightly sweet flavor of the oyster mushrooms. A garnish often sprinkled on Italian stews such as osso bucco, this Milanese seasoning is paired here with pasta to good effect.

3 large garlic cloves, chopped
½ cup chopped fresh flat-leaf parsley
Zest of 2 lemons
1 pound linguine
¼ cup extra-virgin olive oil
2 shallots, minced
8 ounces oyster mushrooms, sliced (2½ cups)
Salt and freshly ground black pepper

Finely mince the garlic, parsley, and lemon zest together until well combined and set aside. Cook the linguine in a large pot of salted boiling water, stirring occasionally, until it is al dente, about 8 minutes. While the pasta is cooking, heat 1 tablespoon of the oil in a large skillet over medium heat. Add the shallots and cook until softened, about 5 minutes. Add the mushrooms and cook, stirring frequently, until they begin to soften, about 3 minutes. Season with salt and pepper to taste. When the pasta is cooked, drain it and place in a large bowl. Add the mushroom mixture, the remaining oil, and the gremolata, and toss gently to combine. Serve immediately.

*Serves 4*

OTHER PASTA CHOICES: fettuccine, spaghetti

# Linguine with Basil Pesto

Eating pasta with pesto can become addictive, so you may want to grow your own basil to keep a supply on hand. I've found you can never have too much pesto, so I like to make large quantities when the basil is at its peak and freeze it in small containers to get me through the winter months. Pesto keeps in the refrigerator for several weeks when topped with a thin layer of olive oil and stored in a tightly sealed container. Note: If you plan to freeze pesto, omit the cheese from the recipe. It can be added after the pesto is defrosted and ready to use.

3 large garlic cloves
½ cup pine nuts
2½ cups fresh basil leaves, firmly packed
½ teaspoon salt
Freshly ground black pepper
½ cup extra-virgin olive oil
¼ cup freshly grated Parmesan or soy Parmesan cheese
1 pound linguine

Combine the garlic and pine nuts in a food processor and pulse until coarsely chopped. Add the basil leaves, salt, and pepper to taste, and blend thoroughly to a paste, scraping down the sides of the bowl as necessary. With the machine running, slowly pour the olive oil through the feed tube and process until well blended. Transfer to a small bowl and stir in the cheese. Set aside. Cook the linguine in a large pot of salted boiling water, stirring occasionally, until it is al dente, about 8 minutes. When the pasta is cooked, drain it and place in a serving bowl. Add the pesto and toss well. Serve immediately.

*Serves 4*

OTHER PASTA CHOICES: fettuccine, spaghetti

# Ziti with Red Pepper–Walnut Pesto

The sweet taste of red bell peppers combines with walnuts and garlic for a rich yet fresh-tasting pesto that can also be used as a colorful spread for crostini or a flavorful dip for vegetables.

1 cup walnut pieces, lightly toasted
1 large red bell pepper, coarsely chopped
2 garlic cloves
¼ cup chopped fresh flat-leaf parsley
½ teaspoon salt
⅛ teaspoon freshly ground black pepper
⅓ cup extra-virgin olive oil
1 pound ziti
Freshly grated Parmesan or soy Parmesan cheese

Place the walnuts, bell pepper, garlic, parsley, salt, and black pepper in a food processor and process until finely chopped. With the machine running, slowly pour the olive oil through the feed tube and process until blended. Set aside. Cook the ziti in a large pot of salted boiling water, stirring occasionally, until it is al dente, about 10 minutes. When the pasta is cooked, drain it and place in a shallow serving bowl. Add the pesto and some grated cheese to taste, and toss well. Serve immediately, with additional grated cheese to pass at the table.

*Serves 4*

OTHER PASTA CHOICES: penne, rigatoni

# Farfalle with Almond-Tarragon Pesto

Although tradition dictates that pesto be served with linguine or other flat strand pasta, the delicate sweetness of almonds and tarragon in this nontraditional pesto reminds me of springtime, so I like to pair it with farfalle, the whimsical "butterfly" pasta, to complete the mood. For an extra touch of spring, add some lightly steamed tender asparagus or early peas.

½ cup whole almonds
2 large garlic cloves
¾ teaspoon salt
2 cups fresh tarragon leaves
Pinch of cayenne pepper
½ cup extra-virgin olive oil
1 pound farfalle

Place the almonds, garlic, and salt in a food processor and pulse until finely ground, about 45 seconds. Add the tarragon and cayenne, and blend thoroughly to a paste, scraping down the sides of the bowl as necessary. With the machine running, slowly pour the olive oil through the feed tube and process until well blended. Set aside. Cook the farfalle in a large pot of salted boiling water, stirring occasionally, until it is al dente, about 8 to 10 minutes. When the pasta is cooked, drain it and place in a serving bowl. Add the pesto and toss well. Serve immediately.

*Serves 4*

OTHER PASTA CHOICES: rotini, radiatore

# Fettuccine with Cilantro-Lime Pesto

The heady Thai-inspired combination of cilantro, lime, and garlic deserves a sturdy pasta such as fettuccine. For extra punch, include a hot chile among the pesto ingredients. For added protein, toss the pasta with stir-fried tofu.

1½ cups fresh cilantro leaves, packed
½ cup fresh flat-leaf parsley, packed
½ cup peanuts
1 large garlic clove
½ teaspoon salt
Pinch of cayenne pepper
Juice and zest of 1 lime
⅓ cup vegetable oil
1 pound fettuccine

Place the cilantro, parsley, peanuts, garlic, salt, and cayenne in a food processor and blend thoroughly to a paste, scraping down the sides of the bowl as necessary. Add the lime juice and zest, and process until blended. With the machine running, slowly pour the oil through the feed tube and process until the mixture is smooth. Set aside. Cook the fettuccine in a large pot of salted boiling water, stirring occasionally, until it is al dente, about 10 minutes. When the pasta is cooked, drain it and place in a serving bowl. Add the pesto and toss well. Serve immediately.

*Serves 4*

OTHER PASTA CHOICES: perciatelli, linguine

# Penne with Roasted Red Pepper Pesto

Using jarred roasted red peppers for this full-flavored pesto saves time, but you can roast two fresh peppers if you prefer. Like several of the other pesto recipes in this chapter, the roasted red pepper pesto is particularly flavorful and well suited to other uses such as a dip for crudités.

2 large garlic cloves
⅓ cup pine nuts
1 (7-ounce) jar roasted red peppers, drained
½ teaspoon salt
Cayenne pepper
¼ cup extra-virgin olive oil
1 pound penne

Place the garlic and pine nuts in a food processor and pulse until coarsely chopped. Add the red peppers, salt, and cayenne pepper to taste, and blend thoroughly to a paste, scraping down the sides of the bowl as necessary. With the machine running, slowly pour the olive oil through the feed tube and process until well blended. Set aside. Cook the penne in a large pot of salted boiling water, stirring occasionally, until it is al dente, about 8 to 10 minutes. When the pasta is cooked, drain it and place in a serving bowl. Add the pesto and toss well. Serve immediately.

*Serves 4*

OTHER PASTA CHOICES: ziti or another tubular pasta

# Angel Hair Pasta with Parsley-Walnut Pesto

Angel hair pasta, or capelli d'angelo, is a very fine spaghetti that is also called capellini. Protein-rich walnuts also contain iron and magnesium, as well as vitamins A, B, and E. Walnuts are a common ingredient in the cuisine of the Italian region of Liguria.

2 cups fresh flat-leaf parsley leaves, packed
¾ cup walnuts
1 large garlic clove, chopped
½ teaspoon salt
Freshly ground black pepper
¼ cup soft or silken tofu
⅓ cup extra-virgin olive oil
1 pound angel hair pasta

Place the parsley, walnuts, garlic, salt, and pepper in a food processor and pulse until coarsely ground. Add the tofu and process until smooth. With the machine running, slowly pour the olive oil through the feed tube and process until well blended. Set aside. Cook the angel hair in large pot of salted boiling water, stirring occasionally, until it is al dente, about 2 to 4 minutes. When the pasta is cooked, drain it and place in a serving bowl. Add the pesto and toss well. Serve immediately.

*Serves 4*

OTHER PASTA CHOICES: vermicelli, spaghettini

# Ziti with Black Olive Tapenade

Use ridged ziti to help ensure that every bit of the flavorful tapenade will cling to the pasta. For the best flavor, be sure to use good quality oil-cured olives for the tapenade—canned black olives packed in water simply won't do.

¼ cup extra-virgin olive oil
1 small onion, minced
2 garlic cloves, chopped
¼ cups oil-cured black olives, pitted
¼ cup chopped fresh flat-leaf parsley
2 tablespoons capers
½ teaspoon salt
¼ teaspoon hot red pepper flakes, or to taste
1 pound ziti

Heat 1 tablespoon of the oil in a skillet over medium heat. Add the onion and garlic. Cover and cook for 5 minutes or until soft. Transfer the mixture to a food processor, add the olives, parsley, capers, salt, and red pepper flakes. Process until the mixture is coarsely blended, about 30 seconds. Set aside. Cook the ziti in a large pot of salted boiling water, stirring occasionally, until it is al dente, about 8 to 10 minutes. When the pasta is cooked, drain it and place in a serving bowl. Add the remaining olive oil and the tapenade and toss well. Serve immediately.

*Serves 4*

OTHER PASTA CHOICES: penne, mostaccioli

# SAUCES AND SHAPES

Although pasta and sauce pairings need not be written in stone, here are guidelines for some tried-and-true combinations:

- Tender, fresh pasta strands complement the creamy sauces of northern Italy

- Heavy, heartier sauces are best with wide noodles or short tubular shapes

- Pasta shapes with crevices or hollows are perfect for capturing bits of a chunky sauce

- Chewy twists stand up to salad dressings and spicy southern Italian sauces

- Smooth, tubular pastas are best with thick, clingy sauces

- Serve long, thin pasta with olive oil sauces and thin tomato sauces

- Dried pasta shapes, popular in southern Italy, are best paired with chunky vegetables

- Pair julienned vegetables with strand pasta

- Serve ridged or ribbed pasta with thinner sauces to help them cling

# Garden Varieties

Pasta and vegetables were made for each other, as evidenced by the tempting assortment of recipes in this chapter that combine the pick of the produce with your favorite pasta shapes. Enjoy summer vegetables at the peak of freshness with delightful dishes such as Grilled Vegetables and Penne (page 42), Orecchiette and Asparagus with Lemon-Tarragon Sauce (page 29), and Zucchini Linguine with Fresh Herbs (page 28).

When vegetables combine with pasta, they can take many forms. Often they will simmer into a chunky mélange, other times they are pureed into a smooth sauce. Or vegetables can be dramatically stir-fried together with the pasta—always complementing, never competing. Whether vegetables are arranged atop a tangle of linguine or tossed with a bowl of penne, the versatile combination of pasta and vegetables is irresistible.

Paglia e Fieno with Green and Yellow Squash

Summer Garden Farfalle

Sage-Scented Ziti with Broccoli, Pine Nuts, and Orange Zest

Zucchini Linguine with Fresh Herbs

Orecchiette and Asparagus with Lemon-Tarragon Sauce

Gemelli with Artichokes and Yellow Pepper Rouille

Penne with Spinach, Pine Nuts, and Raisins

Rigatoni with Radicchio, Italian Peppers, and Leeks

Farfalle with Asparagus and Pine Nuts

Fusilli with Spicy Eggplant, Roasted Red Pepper, and Tomatoes

Spinach Linguine with Cauliflower, Pistachios, and Parsley

Escarole and Beans with Penne

Radiatore with Provençale Vegetables

Ziti with Watercress, Sun-Dried Tomatoes, and Walnuts

Linguine and Root Vegetable Sauté

Grilled Vegetables and Penne

Rapini Rotini

Penne with Sweet Potato and Green Apple Sauté

Mostaccioli and Roasted Vegetables with Salsa Verde

# Paglia e Fieno with Green and Yellow Squash

Tuscany's "straw and hay" pasta dish is so named for its green and yellow noodles. This theme is elaborated on here with the addition of green and yellow squash, cut into long strips with a mandoline slicer. If you don't have a mandoline, a sharp knife or vegetable peeler may be used.

8 ounces spinach linguine
8 ounces regular linguine
¼ cup olive oil
1 zucchini, cut into long, thin strips
1 yellow squash, cut into long, thin strips
Salt and freshly ground black pepper
Freshly grated Parmesan or soy Parmesan cheese

Cook the linguine in a large pot of salted boiling water, stirring occasionally, until it is al dente, about 8 minutes. While the pasta is cooking, heat the oil in a medium skillet over medium heat, add the two squashes, and cook until softened, about 2 minutes. Add salt and pepper to taste and keep warm over low heat. When the pasta is cooked, drain it and place in a serving bowl. Add the squash mixture, sprinkle with cheese, and toss gently to combine. Serve immediately, with extra cheese to pass at the table.

*Serves 4*

OTHER PASTA CHOICES: regular and spinach fettuccine

# Summer Garden Farfalle

A more poetic name for this fresh vegetable and pasta medley would be "Butterflies in the Garden." The mellow, slightly nutty taste of the Asiago cheese complements the natural sweetness of the vegetables, which may be varied according to what's just been picked.

2 tablespoons olive oil
1 red or yellow bell pepper, cut into julienne strips
2 garlic cloves, minced
1 small zucchini, cut into half-rounds
1 small bunch scallions, chopped
Salt and freshly ground black pepper
1 pound farfalle
1 cup small cherry tomatoes, halved
¼ cup minced fresh basil
2 tablespoons minced fresh flat-leaf parsley
Freshly grated Asiago or soy Parmesan cheese

Heat the oil in a large skillet over medium heat, add the bell peppers and garlic, and cook 3 to 5 minutes to soften slightly. Add the zucchini and scallions, and cook 3 minutes longer. Season with salt and pepper to taste and keep warm over low heat. Cook the farfalle in a large pot of salted boiling water, stirring occasionally, until it is al dente, about 8 to 10 minutes. When the pasta is cooked, drain it and place in a large serving bowl. Add the zucchini mixture, along with the tomatoes, basil, and parsley. Sprinkle with cheese, toss gently, and serve immediately.

*Serves 4*

OTHER PASTA CHOICES: cavatappi, rotini

# Sage-Scented Ziti with Broccoli, Pine Nuts, and Orange Zest

Sage, a native Mediterranean herb, is used throughout Italy to add flavor to a number of dishes including the classic Roman sage butter sauce for ravioli. Here sage blends harmoniously with the diverse but complementary flavors of garlic, orange, and pine nuts. If you don't have pine nuts, this dish is also good made with slivered almonds.

> 1 small head broccoli, cut into florets (about 2½ cups)
> ¼ cup extra-virgin olive oil
> ¼ cup pine nuts
> 1 large garlic clove, minced
> 2 tablespoons chopped fresh sage
> Zest and juice of 1 orange
> Salt and freshly ground black pepper
> 1 pound ziti

Lightly steam the broccoli until just tender, about 3 to 5 minutes. Remove from heat and set aside. Heat 1 tablespoon of the oil in a large skillet over medium heat. Add the pine nuts and cook until lightly toasted, about 1 minute. Remove from heat and transfer to a small bowl. Using the same skillet, heat the remaining oil over medium heat. Add the garlic and cook until fragrant and slightly softened, about 30 seconds. Stir in the sage, orange zest, and salt and pepper to taste. Add the orange juice and keep warm over low heat. Cook the ziti in a large pot of salted boiling water, stirring occasionally, until it is al dente, about 8 to 10 minutes. When the pasta is cooked, drain it and place in a large serving bowl. Add the sauce, broccoli, and pine nuts, and toss gently to combine. Serve immediately.

*Serves 4*

OTHER PASTA CHOICES: penne or other tubular pasta

# Zucchini Linguine
# with Fresh Herbs

The bouquet of fresh herbs in this summertime pasta sauté enhances the just-picked flavor of the tender young zucchini. If you don't have the space for an herb garden, consider growing a few pots of fresh herbs on a kitchen windowsill. You will reap the double benefit of fragrant houseplants and enticing culinary ingredients at your fingertips.

¼ cup extra-virgin olive oil
3 to 4 small zucchini, halved lengthwise and thinly sliced
1 small bunch scallions, minced
1 garlic clove, pressed
1 pound linguine
3 tablespoons minced fresh basil
3 tablespoons minced fresh parsley
3 tablespoons snipped fresh chives
Salt and freshly ground black pepper

Heat 1 tablespoon of the oil in a large skillet over medium heat. Add the zucchini, scallions, and garlic, and cook until slightly soft, about 3 to 5 minutes. Keep warm over low heat. Cook the linguine in a large pot of salted boiling water, stirring occasionally, until it is al dente, about 8 minutes. When the pasta is cooked, drain it and place in a large serving bowl. Add the zucchini mixture, the remaining olive oil, the basil, parsley, chives, and salt and pepper to taste. Toss to combine and serve immediately.

*Serves 4*

OTHER PASTA CHOICES: fettuccine, spaghetti

# Orecchiette and Asparagus with Lemon-Tarragon Sauce

Delicate pasta shaped like "little ears" tossed with tender young asparagus and fresh tarragon are a winning springtime combination when fresh, pencil-thin asparagus is plentiful. Orecchiette is a favorite pasta in the Apulia region of Italy, where it is traditionally paired with broccoli rabe.

⅓ cup extra-virgin olive oil
2 garlic cloves, minced
1 pound thin asparagus, cut diagonally into 1-inch pieces
1 pound orecchiette
⅓ cup minced fresh tarragon leaves
Juice and zest of 1 lemon
Salt and freshly ground black pepper

Heat 2 tablespoons of the oil in a large skillet. Add the garlic and asparagus, and cook until the asparagus is just tender, about 5 minutes. Remove from the heat and set aside. Cook the orecchiette in a large pot of salted boiling water, stirring occasionally, until it is al dente, about 8 minutes. When the pasta is cooked, drain it and place in a large serving bowl. Add the asparagus, the remaining olive oil, the tarragon, lemon juice and zest, and salt and pepper to taste. Toss to combine and serve immediately.

*Serves 4*

OTHER PASTA CHOICES: radiatore, or any small pasta shape

# Gemelli with Artichokes and Yellow Pepper Rouille

A rouille is a thick Provençal sauce usually made with roasted red peppers and thickened with bread. This version uses yellow peppers that are sautéed rather than roasted, resulting in a much lighter flavor.

⅓ cup extra-virgin olive oil
2 large yellow bell peppers, coarsely chopped
1 slice firm white bread
½ teaspoon salt
⅛ teaspoon cayenne pepper
1 pound gemelli
2 garlic cloves, pressed
1 (14-ounce) can artichoke hearts, drained and sliced
2 tablespoons chopped fresh basil

Heat 2 tablespoons of the oil in a large skillet over medium-low heat. Add the bell peppers, cover, and cook until very soft, about 15 minutes. Remove from heat. Trim the crusts from the bread and soak in enough water to cover for 5 minutes. Squeeze out the water and place the bread in a food processor along with the bell peppers, salt, and cayenne. Process until smooth and set aside. Cook the gemelli in a large pot of salted boiling water, stirring occasionally, until it is al dente, about 8 to 10 minutes. While the pasta is cooking, heat the remaining oil in a medium skillet. Add the garlic and cook until fragrant, about 30 seconds. Add the artichokes and cook until heated through, stirring to coat them with the garlic and oil. When the pasta is cooked, drain it and place in a large serving bowl. Add the artichokes and toss to combine. Top with the rouille, sprinkle with basil, and serve immediately.

*Serves 4*

OTHER PASTA CHOICES: fusilli, cavatappi

# Penne with Spinach, Pine Nuts, and Raisins

The raisins add a sweet counterpoint to the rest of the dish, especially the touch of hot red pepper. Including raisins and other sweet ingredients in savory recipes is a delicious Sicilian tradition. Adjust the amount of hot pepper flakes used according to personal preference.

1 pound penne
⅓ cup extra-virgin olive oil
2 garlic cloves, minced
1 pound fresh spinach, coarsely chopped
Salt
¼ teaspoon hot red pepper flakes, or to taste
½ cup raisins
¼ cup pine nuts

Cook the penne in a large pot of salted boiling water, stirring occasionally, until it is al dente, about 8 to 10 minutes. While the pasta is cooking, heat 1 tablespoon of the oil in a large skillet over medium heat. Add the garlic, spinach, salt to taste, and red pepper flakes. Cook until the spinach is tender, about 2 to 4 minutes. Add the raisins and pine nuts, and keep warm over low heat. When the pasta is cooked, drain it and place in a large serving bowl. Add the spinach mixture and the remaining oil, and toss to combine. Serve immediately.

*Serves 4*

OTHER PASTA CHOICES: ziti or other tubular pasta

# Rigatoni with Radicchio, Italian Peppers, and Leeks

The slightly bitter flavor of radicchio combines well with the slightly sweet flavor of the peppers and leeks. Leeks have been paired with pasta since ancient times—an early writing of Horace refers to a dish of lasagna and chickpeas made with leeks. They are notorious for retaining sand, so be sure to wash leeks thoroughly before using them.

> ¼ cup extra-virgin olive oil
> 1 leek, white part only, thinly sliced
> 2 or 3 Italian banana peppers, or other mild pepper, thinly sliced
> 8 ounces radicchio, coarsely chopped
> ½ teaspoon salt
> ⅛ teaspoon freshly ground black pepper
> 1 pound rigatoni
> Freshly grated Pecorino Romano or soy Parmesan cheese

Heat 2 tablespoons of the oil in a large skillet over medium heat. Add the leeks and peppers, and cook until soft and slightly browned, about 5 to 7 minutes. Add the radicchio, salt, and pepper, and cook until slightly softened, about 1 minute. Cook the rigatoni in a large pot of salted boiling water, stirring occasionally, until it is al dente, about 8 to 10 minutes. When the pasta is cooked, drain it and place in a large serving bowl. Add the vegetables and the remaining olive oil, and toss to combine. Serve immediately, with a bowl of grated cheese to pass at the table.

*Serves 4*

OTHER PASTA CHOICES: ziti, or another tubular pasta

# Farfalle with Asparagus and Pine Nuts

Lemon and dill provide the sparkle in this fresh-tasting dish that is perfect for spring-time, when tender young asparagus are plentiful. I like to accompany this dish with a bottle of Soave or other crisp Italian white wine.

½ cup pine nuts
3 tablespoons extra-virgin olive oil
1 garlic clove, finely minced
½ pound thin asparagus, cut diagonally into 1-inch pieces
1 pound farfalle
2 tablespoons minced fresh dill
Zest and juice of 1 fresh lemon
Salt and freshly ground black pepper

Lightly toast the pine nuts in a dry skillet over medium heat until golden brown, about 1 to 2 minutes. Transfer the nuts to a small bowl and set aside. Reheat the skillet with 1 tablespoon of the olive oil over medium heat. Add the garlic and asparagus, and cook until the asparagus is slightly tender, about 4 to 5 minutes. Cook the farfalle in large pot of salted boiling water, stirring occasionally, until it is al dente, about 8 to 10 minutes. When the pasta is cooked, drain it and place in a large serving bowl with the asparagus and pine nuts. Add the remaining olive oil, the dill, lemon zest, and lemon juice. Season with salt and pepper to taste, and toss gently to combine. Serve immediately.

*Serves 4*

OTHER PASTA CHOICES: fusilli, gemelli

# Fusilli with Spicy Eggplant, Roasted Red Pepper, and Tomatoes

Pasta and eggplant dishes are popular throughout Sicily, where they are often given the name *pasta alla Norma,* presumably after Bellini's popular opera of the same name. To save time, bottled roasted red peppers may be substituted for fresh.

1 large red bell pepper
1 eggplant, cut into ½-inch dice
2 tablespoons olive oil
Salt
1 small onion, chopped
3 garlic cloves, minced
1 (15-ounce) can diced tomatoes
½ teaspoon hot red pepper flakes, or to taste
1 teaspoon minced fresh oregano, or ½ teaspoon dried
Freshly ground black pepper
½ cup vegetable stock or water
1 pound fusilli
Freshly grated Pecorino Romano or soy Parmesan cheese

Halve and seed the bell pepper and place directly over a gas flame or under the broiler, until the skin is blistered and charred. Place the pepper in a paper or plastic bag and steam for 10 minutes. Rub off the charred skin and coarsely chop. Set aside.

Preheat the oven to 400°F.

Toss the eggplant with 1 tablespoon of the oil and transfer it to a baking sheet. Season the eggplant with salt to taste and roast in the oven for 15 minutes, or until soft, turning once. Remove from the oven and set aside. Heat the remaining tablespoon of oil in large skillet over medium heat. Add the onion and garlic, and cook until soft, about 5 minutes. Reduce heat to low and stir in the tomatoes, roasted eggplant, bell peppers, red pepper flakes, oregano, and salt and black pepper to taste. Simmer for 15 to 20 minutes to blend the flavors. Add the vegetable stock or water if the sauce becomes too thick.

Cook the fusilli in a large pot of salted boiling water, stirring occasionally, until it is al dente, about 8 to 10 minutes. When the pasta is cooked, drain it and place in a large serving bowl. Add the sauce, toss to combine, sprinkle with grated cheese, and serve immediately.

*Serves 4*

OTHER PASTA CHOICES: rotini or other curly pasta

# Spinach Linguine with Cauliflower, Pistachios, and Parsley

The snowy white cauliflower against a backdrop of green noodles makes a striking combination that also tastes great—especially with that surprising crunch and color of the bright green pistachios. Whenever I make this recipe, I buy extra pistachios to snack on or there would never be enough left for cooking.

1 small head cauliflower, broken into small florets
¼ cup extra-virgin olive oil
2 large garlic cloves, pressed
¼ cup minced scallions
Salt and freshly ground black pepper
1 pound spinach linguine
⅓ cup chopped pistachios
¼ cup chopped fresh flat-leaf parsley
Freshly shaved Asiago or grated soy Parmesan cheese

Lightly steam the cauliflower until just tender, about 5 minutes. Remove from heat and set aside. In a large skillet, heat 1 tablespoon of the oil over medium heat. Add the garlic and scallions, and cook until fragrant, about 30 seconds. Add the cauliflower, remaining olive oil, and salt and pepper to taste, and keep warm over low heat. Cook the linguine in a large pot of salted boiling water, stirring occasionally, until it is al dente, about 8 minutes. When the pasta is cooked, drain it and place in a large serving bowl. Add the cauliflower mixture, the pistachios, and parsley. Toss gently and serve immediately, with a bowl of cheese to pass at the table.

*Serves 4*

OTHER PASTA CHOICES: spinach fettuccine

# Escarole and Beans with Penne

This flavorful dish made frequent appearances on the dinner table when I was a child, where I learned early on how delicious "eating my greens" could be. Another dark, leafy green such as chicory (also known as curly endive) may be substituted for the escarole.

3 tablespoons olive oil
3 garlic cloves, crushed
1 head escarole, coarsely chopped and blanched
1½ cups cooked cannellini beans, drained and rinsed
½ teaspoon salt
⅛ teaspoon freshly ground black pepper
1 pound penne

Heat the oil in a large skillet over medium heat. Add the garlic and cook until fragrant, about 30 seconds. Add the escarole and simmer until tender, about 5 minutes. Add the beans, salt, and pepper, and simmer over low heat for about 10 minutes to blend the flavors. Cook the penne in a large pot of salted boiling water, stirring occasionally, until it is al dente, about 8 to 10 minutes. When the pasta is cooked, drain it and place in a large serving bowl. Remove the garlic pieces from the escarole and bean mixture, then add the mixture to the pasta. Toss gently and serve immediately.

*Serves 4*

OTHER PASTA CHOICES: ziti, mostaccioli

# Radiatore with Provençale Vegetables

Although not usually considered a part of French haute cuisine, noodle dishes are popular throughout France, and the classic Provençale vegetable mélange marries perfectly with the chewy radiatore. For a heartier meal, add a can of chickpeas or cannellini beans. Use canned diced tomatoes if fresh are unavailable.

4 ounces fresh green beans, cut into 1-inch pieces
2 tablespoons olive oil
1 small yellow onion, chopped
1 red bell pepper, cut into ¼-inch dice
2 garlic cloves, minced
4 scallions, minced
2 large ripe tomatoes, coarsely chopped
¼ cup minced flat-leaf parsley
1 teaspoon minced fresh marjoram
Salt and freshly ground black pepper
2 tablespoons chopped fresh basil
1 pound radiatore
Freshly shaved Parmesan or grated soy Parmesan cheese

Cook the green beans in boiling water until crisp tender, about 5 minutes. Drain and set aside. Heat the oil in a large skillet over medium heat. Add the onion and bell pepper, and cook until soft, about 5 to 7 minutes. Stir in the garlic and scallions, and cook 1 minute longer. Add the tomatoes, parsley, marjoram, and green beans. Season with salt and pepper to taste, and cook until the vegetables are soft, about 5 to 10 minutes. Stir in the basil and keep warm over low heat. Cook the radiatore in a large pot of salted boiling water, stirring occasionally, until it is al dente, about 8 minutes.

When the pasta is cooked, drain it and place in a large serving bowl. Add the radiatore and vegetables, and toss gently to combine. Top with a small amount of cheese and serve immediately, passing additional cheese at the table.

*Serves 4*

OTHER PASTA CHOICES: orecchiette, farfalle

# Ziti with Watercress, Sun-Dried Tomatoes, and Walnuts

The peppery bite of watercress and the smoky flavor of sun-dried tomatoes punctuate the ziti and walnuts. The optional walnut oil, though expensive, adds a delightful bouquet to the dish. Since it goes rancid quickly, store unused walnut oil in the refrigerator.

    2 tablespoons olive oil
    3 shallots, minced
    1 large bunch watercress, stemmed and coarsely chopped (2½ cups)
    ⅓ cup oil-packed sun-dried tomatoes, drained and chopped
    Salt and freshly ground black pepper
    1 pound ziti
    ½ cup toasted chopped walnuts
    1 tablespoon walnut oil (optional)

Heat the olive oil in a large skillet over medium heat, add the shallots, and cook until slightly soft, about 2 minutes. Add the watercress and stir-fry until just tender, about 3 to 4 minutes. Add the tomatoes, season with salt and pepper to taste, and set aside. Cook the ziti in a large pot of salted boiling water, stirring occasionally, until it is al dente, about 8 to 10 minutes. When the pasta is cooked, drain it and place in a large serving bowl. Add the watercress mixture and toss gently to combine. Sprinkle with the walnuts and drizzle with walnut oil, if you are using it. Serve immediately.

*Serves 4*

OTHER PASTA CHOICES: penne, rigatoni

# Linguine and Root Vegetable Sauté

Although carrots are widely used in the United States, parsnips and rutabagas have never achieved such popularity, perhaps because people don't know what to do with them. This colorful root vegetable sauté, with the rich nuance of toasted pecans, may change all that.

2 carrots, cut diagonally into ¼-inch slices

2 parsnips, cut diagonally into ¼-inch slices

6 ounces rutabaga, peeled and cut into ¼-inch julienne strips

3 tablespoons olive oil

3 shallots, halved

1 teaspoon minced fresh oregano, or ½ teaspoon dried

½ teaspoon minced fresh thyme, or ¼ teaspoon dried

Salt and freshly ground black pepper

1 pound linguine

2 tablespoons minced fresh flat-leaf parsley

⅓ cup chopped pecans, toasted

Steam the carrots, parsnips, and rutabaga until just tender, about 5 minutes. Heat the oil in a large skillet over medium heat. Add the shallots and cook until soft, about 5 minutes. Add the steamed vegetables, oregano, thyme, and salt and pepper to taste. Cook until the vegetables begin to caramelize, about 5 minutes. Cook the linguine in a large pot of salted boiling water, stirring occasionally, until it is al dente, about 8 minutes. When the pasta is cooked, drain it and place in a shallow serving bowl. Add the vegetable mixture and toss gently. Garnish with the parsley and pecans and serve immediately.

*Serves 4*

OTHER PASTA CHOICES: fettuccine, spaghetti

# Grilled Vegetables and Penne

Pasta is perfect anytime—even at a summer cookout, as this dish will attest. Grill some garlic bread and open a bottle of chilled Pinot Grigio for a terrific meal.

1 zucchini, halved lengthwise
1 yellow squash, halved lengthwise
2 portobello mushrooms, stemmed and halved
1 red bell pepper, quartered lengthwise
1 fennel bulb, thinly sliced
4 garlic cloves, unpeeled
4 ripe Roma tomatoes, halved
½ cup olive oil
Salt and freshly ground black pepper
1 pound penne
2 tablespoons minced fresh flat-leaf parsley

Place the vegetables in a bowl with 6 tablespoons of the olive oil and toss to coat.

Prepare the outdoor grill or preheat the oven broiler.

If you are using an oven, arrange the vegetables on a lightly oiled broiler pan. For an outdoor grill, place the vegetables in a mesh or perforated grilling pan. Season the vegetables with salt and pepper to taste, and broil or grill them until they are slightly charred on both sides, turning once. Remove the vegetables from the heat and allow them to cool slightly. Cook the penne in a large pot of salted boiling water, stirring occasionally, until it is al dente, about 8 to 10 minutes. While the pasta is cooking, peel the charred skins from the garlic and cut the cloves in half. Cut the bell pepper, squash, and mushrooms into 1-inch chunks. Keep the vegetables warm in the oven or on the grill. When the pasta is cooked, drain it and place in a large serving bowl. Add the vegetables and the remaining olive oil, and toss gently. Serve immediately, sprinkled with the parsley and some black pepper.

*Serves 4*

OTHER PASTA CHOICES: ziti, rigatoni

# Rapini Rotini

Also called broccoli rabe, rapini is an assertive green that stands up to the garlic and olives. It is a popular vegetable throughout Italy, especially in the Apulia region, where it is traditionally paired with orecchiette. For a more substantial dish, add a can of cannellini beans.

8 ounces fresh rapini
¼ cup extra-virgin olive oil
1 garlic clove, minced
Salt
¼ teaspoon hot red pepper flakes
⅓ cup oil-cured black olives, pitted
1 pound rotini
Freshly grated Parmesan or soy Parmesan cheese

Trim the thick stems from the rapini and coarsely chop. Blanch for 2 minutes, drain, and set aside. Heat 2 tablespoons of the oil in a large skillet over medium heat. Add the garlic and cook until fragrant, about 30 seconds. Add the rapini, salt to taste, and red pepper flakes. Cook, stirring frequently, until the rapini is tender, about 5 minutes. Add the olives and keep warm over low heat. Cook the rotini in a large pot of salted boiling water, stirring occasionally, until it is al dente, about 8 to 10 minutes. When the pasta is cooked, drain it and place in a large serving bowl. Add the rapini and remaining olive oil, and toss to combine. Serve immediately, with a bowl of grated cheese to pass at the table.

*Serves 4*

OTHER PASTA CHOICES: rotelle or other curly pasta

# Penne with Sweet Potato and Green Apple Sauté

This surprising combination of sweet potatoes, apples, and raisins makes an interesting change from the normal pasta routine. The toasted pecans add texture and flavor to this colorful autumn dish.

3 tablespoons olive oil
1 small yellow onion, thinly sliced
1 large sweet potato, peeled and cut into ½-inch dice
1 large Granny Smith apple, cored and thinly sliced
¼ cup chopped golden raisins
Salt and freshly ground black pepper
1 pound penne
¼ cup chopped pecans, toasted

Heat 2 tablespoons of the oil in a large skillet over medium heat. Add the onion and sweet potato, and cook, covered, until the potato softens, about 8 to 10 minutes. Add the apple, raisins, and salt and pepper to taste, and cook 3 to 5 minutes longer or until the apple softens. Keep warm over low heat. Cook the penne in a large pot of salted boiling water, stirring occasionally, until it is al dente, about 8 to 10 minutes. When the pasta is cooked, drain it and place in a large serving bowl. Add the sweet potato and apple mixture and the remaining olive oil, and toss gently to combine. Garnish with the pecans and serve immediately.

*Serves 4*

OTHER PASTA CHOICES: any tubular pasta but farfalle is nice, too

# Mostaccioli and Roasted Vegetables with Salsa Verde

Roasting vegetable in a hot oven brings out their natural sweetness and adds a deep, rich flavor. I usually make this dish on a cold winter day, so the heat of the oven can warm the kitchen as the fragrance of roasting vegetables permeates the house.

2 small zucchini, halved lengthwise and cut into ¼-inch slices
1 red or yellow bell pepper, cut into ½-inch dice
1 small eggplant, cut into ½-inch dice
4 plum tomatoes, quartered
3 garlic cloves, halved
3 tablespoons olive oil
1 teaspoon dried basil
½ teaspoon dried oregano
Salt and freshly ground black pepper
1 pound mostaccioli
½ cup Salsa Verde (recipe follows)

Preheat the oven to 400°F.

Combine the zucchini, bell pepper, eggplant, tomatoes, garlic, and olive oil in a large baking dish and toss to coat. Sprinkle with the basil, oregano, and salt and pepper to taste, and roast for 30 to 40 minutes, stirring occasionally, until the vegetables are soft and slightly browned around the edges. When the vegetables are done, turn the oven off, and keep them warm in the oven. Cook the mostaccioli in a large pot of salted boiling water, stirring occasionally, until it is al dente, about 8 to 10 minutes. When the pasta is cooked, drain it and place in a large serving bowl. Add the vegetables and salsa verde, and toss to combine. Serve immediately.

*Serves 4*

OTHER PASTA CHOICES: ziti or any tubular pasta

# Salsa Verde

Similar to a pesto, this fresh-tasting green sauce adds a touch of piquancy to the roasted vegetables. Although parsley and basil are traditional, feel free to experiment with other fresh herbs.

⅓ cup fresh flat-leaf parsley leaves, tightly packed
⅓ cup fresh basil leaves, tightly packed
1 large garlic clove
1 tablespoon capers
2 tablespoons balsamic vinegar
½ teaspoon salt
⅛ teaspoon freshly ground black pepper
½ cup extra-virgin olive oil

In a food processor, blend all the ingredients except the oil until finely ground. With the machine running, slowly pour the olive oil through the feed tube and process until well blended.

*Makes about 1¼ cups*

# PLATE OR BOWL?

For a classic Italian presentation of a pasta dish, serve it family-style in a large shallow serving bowl placed directly on the table for passing. This works well for family dining or for casual entertaining. For a more formal, sophisticated look, you may prefer to assemble individual plates or bowls in the kitchen. This option allows for garnishing, if desired, and it is easier to serve. It also reduces the chance of pasta sauce dripping onto your good tablecloth.

But should pasta be eaten from flat plates or shallow soup bowls? The answer is "either," and it is best decided according to individual circumstance and preference. Pasta eaten from shallow soup bowls can be easier to maneuver with a fork and is thought to keep the pasta warmer than on a flat plate. Still, it is also perfectly acceptable to pile pasta directly onto plates. Some people prefer to serve the saucier pasta dishes in bowls and leave the chunkier presentations for the plates. Ultimately, the choice is yours.

# You Say Tomato

When tomatoes were first introduced to Italy from the New World, people thought they were poisonous and were reluctant to eat them. Thankfully, Italian cooks eventually began to incorporate tomatoes in their cooking and today perhaps the most popular way to sauce pasta is with a classic red tomato sauce.

Yet, while most tomato-based sauces have certain similarities, there is also a wide degree of variation among them. In this chapter we will explore some of those variations, including a baked tomato sauce, an uncooked tomato sauce, and a rich tomato pesto.

Not to be missed are regional Italian tomato favorites such as Ziti with Sicilian-Style Tomato Sauce (page 55), a robust sauce made with eggplant, capers, and garlic, and other classic recipes such as Pasta Puttanesca (page 58), Arrabbiata Sauce and Mushrooms over Penne (page 57), and Spaghetti with Red Gravy (page 51).

A tomato sauce is only as good as its ingredients, and fresh ripe tomatoes are often scarce. Fortunately, there are a number of high-quality tomato products on the market, including pastes, purees, and whole and diced tomatoes. These are the products to use when fresh tomatoes are not available. In addition to producing excellent results, they can be great timesavers.

Spaghetti with Red Gravy

Fresh Tomato and Fennel Sauce over Linguine

Cavatelli with Tomato and Red Bell Pepper Sauce

Ziti with Sicilian-Style Tomato Sauce

Fusilli with Uncooked Tomato Sauce

Arrabbiata Sauce and Mushrooms over Penne

Pasta Puttanesca

Spaghettini with Tomato Pesto

Rigatoni with Baked Tomato Sauce

Tricolor Radiatore with Three-Tomato Sauce

Small Shells with Chunky Tomato Sauce

Fusilli with Tomato-Mushroom Sauce

Fettuccine with Creamy Tomato Sauce

Spaghetti with Classic Red

# Spaghetti with Red Gravy

In my family, red pasta sauce was referred to as "gravy." Like my mother's smooth rich sauce, this recipe calls for a high-quality tomato paste that is "fried" to mellow out the flavor.

1 tablespoon olive oil
1 onion, halved
1 large garlic clove, crushed
1 (6-ounce) can tomato paste
½ teaspoon dried oregano
1½ cups hot water
1 (15-ounce) can tomato puree
¼ cup dry red wine
1 bay leaf
Salt and freshly ground black pepper
1 pound spaghetti
Freshly grated Pecorino Romano or soy Parmesan cheese

Heat the oil in a large saucepan over medium heat. Add the onion and garlic, and cook until fragrant, about 1 minute, being careful not to burn the garlic. Add the tomato paste and oregano, and cook, stirring, for 1 minute to heat through. Stir in the water, blending until smooth. Add the tomato puree, wine, and bay leaf, and bring to a boil. Reduce heat to low, season with salt and pepper to taste, and simmer for about 30 minutes or until the sauce thickens. Taste to adjust the seasonings, and remove the onion, garlic, and bay leaf before serving. Cook the spaghetti in a large pot of salted boiling water, stirring occasionally, until it is al dente, about 8 minutes. When the pasta is cooked, drain it and place in a large shallow serving bowl or individual plates. Ladle the sauce over the pasta, sprinkle with cheese, and serve, passing a bowl of grated cheese at the table.

*Serves 4*

OTHER PASTA CHOICES: linguine or other strand pasta

# Fresh Tomato and Fennel Sauce over Linguine

This sauce is best made with very ripe tomatoes that are complemented by the faintly licorice flavor of fresh fennel, a popular vegetable in Italian cooking. When eaten raw, fennel is said to aid digestion. If you want to make this sauce when tomatoes are out of season, substitute high-quality canned tomatoes. San Marzano tomatoes, imported from Italy, are especially good.

2 pounds fresh ripe tomatoes
2 tablespoons olive oil
1 yellow onion, minced
1 fennel bulb, thinly sliced
1 large garlic clove, minced
2 tablespoons tomato paste
½ cup vegetable stock or hot water
1 tablespoon chopped fresh basil, or 1 teaspoon dried
1 teaspoon minced fresh oregano, or ¼ teaspoon dried
1 teaspoon salt
Freshly ground black pepper
1 pound linguine
Freshly grated Parmesan or soy Parmesan cheese

Cut an "**x**" on the bottom of each tomato with a sharp knife and plunge in boiling water for 30 seconds. Remove from water and peel off the skins. Coarsely chop the tomatoes and set aside. Heat the oil in a large saucepan over medium heat. Add the onion, fennel, and garlic. Cover and cook, stirring occasionally, until soft, about 5 minutes. Remove lid. Stir in the tomato paste, tomatoes, vegetable stock or water, and bring to a boil. If using dried herbs, add them now. Reduce heat to low, add the salt, and pepper to taste, and simmer for about 30 minutes or until a thick, rich consistency is reached. If using fresh basil and oregano, stir in at this time. Adjust the seasonings to taste and keep warm over low heat. Cook the linguine in a large pot of salted boiling water, stirring occasionally, until it is al dente, about 8 minutes. When the pasta is cooked, drain it and place in a large shallow serving bowl or individual plates. Ladle the sauce over the pasta and serve with grated cheese.

Serves 4

OTHER PASTA CHOICES: fettuccine, spaghetti

# Cavatelli with Tomato and Red Bell Pepper Sauce

The fresh full-bodied flavor of the bell peppers in this rich tomato sauce complements the chewy texture of the cavatelli. Look for frozen cavatelli at Italian grocery stores, specialty food stores, or well-stocked supermarkets. To me, the frozen are nearly as good as fresh, while dried cavatelli are a pale comparison, and similar in name only.

2 tablespoons olive oil
1 onion, coarsely chopped
1½ pounds red bell peppers, coarsely chopped
½ cup hot vegetable stock or hot water
Salt and freshly ground black pepper
2 tablespoons chopped fresh basil, or 1½ teaspoons dried
1 (16-ounce) can tomato puree
1 pound frozen cavatelli
Freshly grated Parmesan or soy Parmesan cheese

Heat the olive oil in a large skillet over medium heat. Add the onion and peppers, cover, and cook, stirring occasionally, until the vegetables are soft, about 10 minutes. Add the vegetable stock or water, and salt and pepper to taste. Simmer for 5 minutes longer, then transfer the mixture to a food processor. Add the basil and process until smooth. Transfer the sauce to a saucepan, stir in the tomato puree and simmer over medium heat to combine the flavors and reduce slightly, about 10 minutes. Meanwhile, cook the cavatelli in a large pot of salted boiling water, stirring occasionally, until it is chewy but still firm, about 8 minutes. When the pasta is cooked, drain it and place in a large shallow serving bowl or individual plates. Ladle the sauce over the pasta and serve, passing a bowl of grated cheese at the table.

*Serves 4*

OTHER PASTA CHOICES: dried cavatelli, gnocchi

# Ziti with Sicilian-Style Tomato Sauce

Look for ziti rigate, or ridged ziti—the chunky sauce will adhere better than it will to the smooth variety. The addition of eggplant adds hearty texture to the rich sauce and makes it distinctly Sicilian.

2 tablespoons olive oil
1 small eggplant, cut into ½-inch dice
1 small red bell pepper, cut into ½-inch dice
1 large garlic clove, pressed
2 tablespoons tomato paste
1 (29-ounce) can diced tomatoes
1 tablespoon capers, drained
Salt and freshly ground black pepper
¼ cup chopped fresh basil, or 2 teaspoons dried
1 pound ziti
Freshly grated Pecorino Romano or soy Parmesan cheese

Heat the olive oil in a large skillet over medium heat. Add the eggplant and cook, stirring occasionally, until lightly browned, about 10 minutes. Add the bell pepper and garlic, and cook until softened, about 5 minutes. Stir in the tomato paste, tomatoes, capers, and salt and black pepper to taste, and bring to a boil. Reduce the heat to low and simmer for 15 minutes to reduce slightly and blend the flavors. Add the basil and keep warm over low heat. Cook the ziti in a large pot of salted boiling water, stirring occasionally, until it is al dente, about 8 to 10 minutes. When the pasta is cooked, drain it and place in a shallow serving bowl. Add the sauce, sprinkle with grated cheese, and toss gently. Serve immediately, with additional grated cheese to pass at the table.

*Serves 4*

OTHER PASTA CHOICES: penne, rigatoni

# Fusilli with Uncooked Tomato Sauce

Quality ingredients are the key to this summertime favorite. Be sure to use extra-virgin olive oil and only the freshest, ripest tomatoes. This easy sauce is terrific served with either hot or cold pasta, and it makes a good addition to a buffet since it doesn't need to be kept warm.

2 pounds ripe tomatoes, coarsely chopped (about 4 cups)
1 garlic clove, minced
¼ cup extra-virgin olive oil
¼ cup chopped fresh basil
Salt and freshly ground black pepper
1 pound fusilli
Freshly shaved Parmesan or soy Parmesan cheese

Place the tomatoes in a large bowl. Add the garlic, oil, basil, and salt and pepper to taste. Stir gently to combine. Cover, and let stand at room temperature for 30 to 45 minutes to allow the flavors to blend. Stir occasionally. Meanwhile, cook the fusilli in a large pot of salted boiling water, stirring occasionally, until it is al dente, about 8 to 10 minutes. When the pasta is cooked, drain it and place in a shallow serving bowl. Add the sauce and toss gently to combine. Serve immediately, or, if serving cold, refrigerate until close to serving time, but allow to come to room temperature before serving. Top with a few shavings of cheese, passing additional cheese separately.

*Serves 4*

OTHER PASTA CHOICES: cavatappi or other curly pasta

# Arrabbiata Sauce and Mushrooms over Penne

Literally meaning "enraged" or "angry," this Roman classic is named for its fiery flavor derived from the small red chiles called peperoncino that are used to make the sauce. If dried chiles are unavailable, substitute hot red pepper flakes, using more or less according to taste. Mushrooms, while not traditional to the sauce, add substance and flavor.

2 tablespoons olive oil

8 ounces white mushrooms, chopped

2 large garlic cloves, minced

1 or 2 dried red chiles, crumbled, or 1 teaspoon hot red pepper flakes

8 to 10 ripe plum tomatoes, or 1 (28-ounce) can with their juice, chopped

Salt and freshly ground black pepper

1 pound penne

Freshly grated Parmesan or soy Parmesan cheese

2 tablespoons minced fresh basil

Heat the oil in a large skillet over medium heat. Add the mushrooms, garlic, and chiles, and cook until the vegetables soften, about 5 minutes. Add the tomatoes and salt and pepper to taste. Simmer for 15 minutes to allow the flavors to blend. Cook the penne in salted boiling water, stirring occasionally, until it is al dente, about 8 to 10 minutes. When the pasta is cooked, drain it and place in a large serving bowl. Add the sauce, a sprinkling of cheese, and half the basil. Toss gently to combine. Top with the remaining basil and serve immediately, with additional cheese to pass at the table.

*Serves 4*

OTHER PASTA CHOICES: ziti or other tubular pasta

# Pasta Puttanesca

Explanations for the name vary: Some say this "streetwalker style" pasta dish is so named because the sauce is too good to resist. Another story relates that it was a quick meal that the ladies of the evening could easily prepare from pantry ingredients after a hard night's work. No cheese is necessary with this extraordinarily flavorful sauce.

2 tablespoons olive oil
3 large garlic cloves, finely chopped
½ teaspoon hot red pepper flakes, or to taste
2 tablespoons tomato paste
1 (29-ounce) can diced tomatoes
1 cup pitted black gaeta olives, halved
2 tablespoons capers, rinsed and drained
1 teaspoon dried basil
Salt and freshly ground black pepper
1 pound spaghetti
2 tablespoons minced fresh flat-leaf parsley

Heat the oil in a large saucepan over medium heat. Add the garlic and red pepper flakes and cook until fragrant, about 30 seconds. Stir in the tomato paste, tomatoes, olives, capers, and basil. Season with salt and pepper to taste. Bring the sauce to a boil, then reduce heat to low and simmer for 10 minutes, stirring occasionally. Cook the spaghetti in a large pot of salted boiling water, stirring occasionally, until it is al dente, about 8 minutes. When the pasta is cooked, drain it and place in a large serving bowl. Add the sauce and toss gently to combine. Sprinkle with minced parsley and serve immediately.

*Serves 4*

OTHER PASTA CHOICES: linguine, perciatelli

# Spaghettini with Tomato Pesto

Smoky sun-dried tomatoes add a depth of flavor to the fresh-tasting plum tomatoes and basil. This pesto can also be used to make a delicious stuffing for baked stuffed mushrooms. Simply combine the pesto with chopped mushroom stems and bread-crumbs, stuff into the mushroom caps, and bake until done.

> 4 garlic cloves, chopped
> ¼ cup pine nuts
> ½ teaspoon salt
> 6 fresh ripe plum tomatoes, coarsely chopped
> ½ cup oil-packed sun-dried tomatoes, chopped
> ¼ cup chopped fresh basil
> ⅓ cup extra-virgin olive oil
> 1 pound spaghettini

Place the garlic, pine nuts, and salt in a food processor and blend thoroughly to a paste, scraping down the sides of the bowl as necessary. Add the fresh and sun-dried tomatoes and half the basil, and process until well blended. With the machine running, slowly pour the oil through the feed tube and process until blended. Cook the spaghettini in a large pot of salted boiling water, stirring occasionally, until it is al dente, about 2 to 4 minutes. When the pasta is cooked, drain it and place in a large serving bowl. Add the pesto and toss gently to combine. Sprinkle with the remaining basil and serve immediately.

*Serves 4*

OTHER PASTA CHOICES: capellini, vermicelli

# Rigatoni with Baked Tomato Sauce

Baking the tomatoes brings out their natural sweetness and intensifies their flavor. Use only the large, red vine-ripened tomatoes for this recipe.

6 to 8 large ripe tomatoes, cored
2 tablespoons olive oil
¾ teaspoon salt
½ teaspoon sugar
Freshly ground black pepper
3 large garlic cloves, crushed
1 tablespoon minced fresh basil, or 1 teaspoon dried
1 teaspoon minced fresh oregano, or ¼ teaspoon dried
1 pound rigatoni
Freshly grated Parmesan or soy Parmesan cheese

Preheat the oven to 450°F.

Place the tomatoes in a lightly oiled shallow baking dish and drizzle the oil over them. Sprinkle the tomatoes with the salt, sugar, and pepper to taste, and bake  minutes. Reduce the oven temperature to 375°, add the garlic, and bake for 30 to 40 minutes longer, or until the tomatoes are very soft. Remove from the oven and allow to cool. Carefully remove the skins from the tomatoes and discard (they should slip off easily). Transfer the tomatoes and garlic to a food processor and process until smooth. Strain the tomato mixture into a saucepan. Add the basil and oregano. If the sauce is too thin, bring it to a boil and simmer until the liquid is reduced. Otherwise, heat the sauce and adjust the seasonings to taste. Cook the rigatoni in a large pot of salted boiling water, stirring occasionally, until it is al dente, about 8 to 10 minutes. When the pasta is cooked, drain it and place in a serving bowl. Add the sauce, sprinkle with cheese, and toss to combine. Serve immediately.

*Serves 4*

OTHER PASTA CHOICES: ziti, penne

# Tricolor Radiatore with Three-Tomato Sauce

This sauce has extra-rich tomato flavor courtesy of three kinds of tomatoes. Although we often associate pasta with tomato sauce, the combination is relatively recent, since the tomato, which is indigenous to the Americas, came into common use in Italy only in the 1700s.

2 tablespoons olive oil
2 large garlic cloves, finely minced
6 fresh ripe plum tomatoes, coarsely chopped
½ cup oil-packed sun-dried tomatoes, chopped
1 (15-ounce) can diced tomatoes, drained
¼ cup chopped fresh basil, or 1 teaspoon dried
Salt and freshly ground black pepper
1 pound tricolor radiatore
Freshly grated Parmesan or soy Parmesan cheese

Heat the oil in a large saucepan over medium heat. Add the garlic and cook until fragrant, about 30 seconds. Add the fresh, sun-dried, and canned tomatoes to the saucepan and cook, stirring occasionally, about 10 minutes. Stir in the dried basil if you are using it, and salt and pepper to taste. Reduce the heat to low and simmer for 15 minutes to blend the flavors. If you are using fresh basil, stir it in now. Keep the sauce warm over low heat. Cook the radiatore in a large pot of salted boiling water, stirring occasionally, until it is al dente, about 8 minutes. When the pasta is cooked, drain it and place in a shallow serving bowl. Add the sauce, sprinkle with some grated cheese, and toss gently. Serve immediately, with additional grated cheese to pass at the table.

*Serves 4*

OTHER PASTA CHOICES: orecchiette, farfalle

# Small Shells with Chunky Tomato Sauce

Small shells, also called conchiglie, are the perfect pasta shape for holding bits of the chunky sauce. Here a *battuto,* a chopped raw vegetable mixture, is used as a starting point for the rich sauce. Usually consisting of onion, carrots, and celery, once the *battuto* has been cooked, it is referred to as a *soffrito.* The French term for this mixture, whether raw or cooked, is a *mirepoix.*

1 tablespoon olive oil
1 yellow onion, chopped
1 carrot, finely chopped
1 stalk celery, minced
1 large garlic clove, minced
2 pounds fresh ripe tomatoes, or 2 (15-ounce) cans diced tomatoes
¼ cup dry red wine
1 tablespoon chopped fresh basil, or 1 teaspoon dried
1 teaspoon minced fresh oregano, or ¼ teaspoon dried
1 teaspoon sugar (optional)
Salt and freshly ground black pepper
1 pound small shells
Freshly grated Parmesan or soy Parmesan cheese

Heat the oil in a large saucepan over medium heat. Add the onion, carrot, celery, and garlic. Cover and cook, stirring occasionally, until softened, about 5 to 7 minutes. Remove lid. If using fresh tomatoes, cut an "X" on the bottom of each tomato with a sharp knife and plunge into boiling water for 30 seconds. Remove from the water and peel off the skins. Coarsely chop the tomatoes and add to the saucepan. If using canned tomatoes, add them now, along with the wine and the dried basil, oregano, and sugar, if you are using them. Bring to a boil, reduce heat to low, season with salt and pepper to taste, and simmer for about 30 minutes or until a thick, rich consistency is reached. If using fresh basil and oregano, stir in at this time. Cook the shells in a large pot of salted boiling water, stirring occasionally, until they are al dente, about 8 minutes. When the pasta is cooked, drain it and place in a large shallow serving bowl. Add the sauce and toss gently to combine. Serve immediately, with a bowl of grated cheese to pass at the table.

*Serves 4*

OTHER PASTA CHOICES: orecchiette, rigatoni

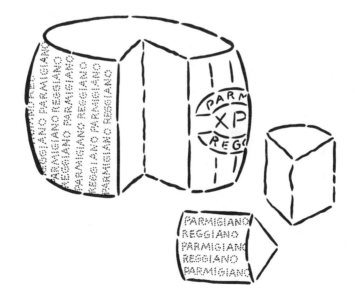

# Fusilli with Tomato-Mushroom Sauce

For a deeper, more woodsy flavor, eliminate the white mushrooms and use all porcini instead. As another alternative, use one ounce of dried porcini for an even more intense flavor. Reconstitute dried porcini in warm water for twenty minutes before using in the recipe.

2 tablespoons olive oil
2 large garlic cloves, minced
4 ounces porcini mushrooms, chopped
4 ounces white mushrooms, chopped
1 (29-ounce) can plum tomatoes, drained and chopped
1 teaspoon dried marjoram
Salt and freshly ground black pepper
1 pound fusilli
Freshly shaved or grated Parmesan or soy Parmesan cheese

Heat the oil in a large skillet over medium heat. Add the garlic and both kinds of mushrooms, and cook until the vegetables soften, about 5 minutes. Add the tomatoes, marjoram, and salt and pepper to taste. Simmer for 15 minutes to blend the flavors. Cook the fusilli in salted boiling water, stirring occasionally, until it is al dente, about 8 to 10 minutes. When the pasta is cooked, drain it and place in a large serving bowl. Add the sauce, and toss gently to combine. Top with a sprinkling of cheese and serve immediately.

*Serves 4*

OTHER PASTA CHOICES: **gemelli, cavatappi**

# Fettuccine with Creamy Tomato Sauce

Tofu provides added protein along with a creamy texture in this rich-tasting sauce. A good-quality canned tomato is imperative to the success of this sauce—imported Italian brands tend to be more flavorful.

1 tablespoon olive oil
1 small yellow onion, finely minced
1 garlic clove, pressed
1 (29-ounce) can diced tomatoes
1 teaspoon dried basil
1/2 teaspoon dried marjoram
Salt and freshly ground black pepper
¼ cup soft or silken tofu
1 pound fettuccine
2 tablespoons minced fresh flat-leaf parsley

Heat the oil in a large saucepan over medium heat. Add the onion and cook until soft, about 5 minutes. Stir in the garlic, tomatoes, basil, marjoram, and salt and pepper to taste. Bring the sauce to a boil, then reduce heat to low and simmer for 20 minutes, stirring occasionally, to blend the flavors and reduce slightly. Place the tofu in a blender or food processor with the sauce and process until smooth. Return to the saucepan and adjust the seasonings to taste. Keep the sauce warm over low heat. Cook the fettuccine in a large pot of salted boiling water, stirring occasionally, until al dente, about 10 minutes. When the pasta is cooked, drain it and place in a large serving bowl. Add the sauce and toss to combine. Sprinkle with the parsley and serve immediately.

*Serves 4*

OTHER PASTA CHOICES: linguine, pappardelle

# Spaghetti with Classic Red

The classic spaghetti and tomato sauce is traditionally Italian and naturally vegetarian. A small amount of sugar is added to the sauce to counteract the acidity of the tomato paste.

1 tablespoon olive oil
1 yellow onion, chopped
2 garlic cloves, pressed
¼ cup tomato paste
1 teaspoon sugar
1 teaspoon dried oregano
1 teaspoon dried basil
¼ cup dry red wine
1 (29-ounce) can crushed tomatoes
Salt and freshly ground black pepper
1 pound spaghetti
2 tablespoons minced fresh flat-leaf parsley
Freshly grated Parmesan or soy Parmesan cheese

Heat the oil in a large saucepan over medium heat. Add the onion and cook until soft, about 5 minutes. Stir in the garlic, tomato paste, sugar, oregano, and basil. Stir in the wine. Add the tomatoes and salt and pepper to taste. Bring the sauce to a boil, then reduce heat to low and simmer for 20 to 25 minutes, stirring occasionally. For a smooth sauce, pass it through a strainer to remove the solids, then return to the saucepan. Keep the sauce warm over low heat. Meanwhile, cook the spaghetti in a large pot of salted boiling water, stirring occasionally, until it is al dente, about 8 minutes. When the pasta is cooked, drain it and place in a large serving bowl. Add the sauce and toss gently to combine. Sprinkle with the parsley and a light dusting of cheese, and serve immediately, with additional cheese to pass at the table.

*Serves 4*

OTHER PASTA CHOICES: linguine, perciatelli

# TWIRLING TIPS

Spaghetti, linguine, and other strand pastas are traditionally eaten with a single fork, twirling a small amount at a time around the fork's tines. To eat pasta like a pro, entwine just a few strands on your fork and twirl two or three times to produce a compact forkful of pasta that can be raised to the mouth. Although most Italians shun the idea of enlisting the aid of a soup spoon to help with the twirling, it does help get the job done. Don't worry if a few short pasta strands are left hanging. Part of the fun of eating pasta is becoming skilled at getting it into your mouth. However, if slurping spaghetti is just not your style, there's only one solution: Choose one of the smaller pasta shapes that are not so unwieldy so you can eat more demurely. For whenever there is a tangle of pasta strands, there is bound to be some slurping.

# Creamy Yet Light

With the exception of fettuccine Alfredo, which originated in Rome, most traditional cream sauces hail from the northern regions of Italy, where they are enjoyed with fresh pasta.

If you have banished pasta dishes made with creamy sauces as unhealthy indulgences, these recipes will put them back in your good graces. Now, rich creamy pasta sauces can actually be good for you when they are made with healthful soy products or pureed beans and vegetables, instead of loaded down with heavy cream, butter, and cheese. Some of these recipes employ just a sprinkling of grated cheese to finish the dish with great taste and a fraction of the fat and calories.

Enjoy satisfying recipes such as Penne with Winter Vegetable Sauce (page 72), Tahini Rotini with Broccoli and Lemon (page 74) and, of course, an updated version of Alfredo's famous fettuccine (page 71).

Alfredo's Fettuccine Revisited

Penne with Winter Vegetable Sauce

Rotelle with Spicy Pumpkin Sauce

Tahini Rotini with Broccoli and Lemon

Fettuccine with Creamy Mushroom and Green Peppercorn Sauce

Penne with Artichokes and Oyster Mushrooms

Spaghettini with Creamy Garlic-Sage Sauce

Conchiglie and Peas with Red Pepper Coulis

Penne with Vodka-Tomato Sauce

Linguine with Summer Vegetable Puree

Perciatelli with Brandy-Cashew Cream

Fettuccine with Sage-Cannellini Puree

# Alfredo's Fettuccine Revisited

Cashews and soy are used to enrich this heart-healthy version of the classic cream sauce. The original high-cholesterol dish was created in Rome by a restaurateur named Alfredo, who tossed it with gold-plated forks.

1 tablespoon olive oil
1 small yellow onion, chopped
½ cup raw cashews
½ cup soft or silken tofu
2 cups milk or soy milk
⅓ cup freshly grated Parmesan or soy Parmesan cheese,
    plus extra for the table
Salt and freshly ground white pepper
1 pound fresh or dried fettuccine
2 tablespoons minced fresh flat-leaf parsley

Heat the oil in a large skillet over medium heat, add the onion, cover, and cook until very soft, about 7 or 8 minutes. In a food processor, finely grind the cashews, then add the onion and process to a paste. Add the tofu and soy milk, and process until well blended. Transfer the mixture to a saucepan, stir in the grated cheese and salt and white pepper to taste, and keep warm over very low heat. Cook the fettuccine in a large pot of salted boiling water until it is al dente, about 3 to 4 minutes for fresh or about 10 minutes for dried. When the pasta is cooked, drain it and place in a shallow serving bowl. Add the sauce and toss to combine. Divide the pasta among individual plates or keep in the serving bowl, and sprinkle with the parsley. Serve immediately, with additional cheese to pass at the table.

*Serves 4*

OTHER PASTA CHOICES: pappardelle, linguine

# Penne with Winter Vegetable Sauce

Northern Italians favor fresh pasta ribbons such as linguine and fettuccine to host their rich cream sauces, but I like to use different dried pasta shapes to catch every drop of this rich sauce, made creamy with pureed vegetables.

1 tablespoon olive oil
1 yellow onion, chopped
2 carrots, chopped
1 stalk celery, chopped
1 red bell pepper, chopped
2 garlic cloves, crushed
1 (14-ounce) can diced tomatoes
1 teaspoon dried savory
Salt and freshly ground black pepper
1 pound penne
Minced fresh flat-leaf parsley

Heat the oil in a large saucepan over medium heat. Add the onion, carrots, celery, bell pepper, and garlic. Cover and cook 10 minutes, stirring occasionally. Add the tomatoes, savory, and salt and pepper to taste, and cook 5 minutes longer. Place the vegetable mixture in a food processor and puree, then transfer back to the saucepan and simmer over low heat for 10 minutes. Adjust the seasonings, adding a little stock or water if the mixture becomes too thick. Cook the penne in a large pot of salted boiling water, stirring occasionally, until it is al dente, about 8 to 10 minutes. When the pasta is cooked, drain it and place in a shallow serving bowl. Add the sauce, sprinkle with the parsley, and serve immediately.

*Serves 4*

OTHER PASTA CHOICES: ziti, rigatoni

# Rotelle with Spicy Pumpkin Sauce

This vivid orange sauce is especially fun at Halloween, when you might consider a strikingly festive garnish of chopped black olives. Canned pumpkin cuts down on preparation time, but fresh pumpkin or winter squash may be used instead.

1 tablespoon olive oil
1 small yellow onion, minced
1 small red bell pepper, chopped
1 garlic clove, minced
1 (15-ounce) can pumpkin
½ cup vegetable stock or water
1 tablespoon cornstarch
¾ teaspoon salt
¼ teaspoon allspice
⅛ teaspoon cayenne pepper, or to taste
½ cup milk or soy milk
1 pound rotelle

Heat the oil in a large skillet over medium heat. Add the onion, bell pepper, and garlic, and cook for 10 minutes or until soft. Transfer the vegetable mixture to a food processor and puree. Add the pumpkin, stock or water, cornstarch, salt, allspice, and cayenne, and process until smooth. Transfer to a saucepan, stir in the milk or soy milk, and heat to a simmer, stirring constantly for 5 minutes to thicken. Adjust the seasonings to taste, and keep warm over very low heat. Cook the rotelle in a large pot of salted boiling water, stirring occasionally, until it is al dente, about 8 to 10 minutes. When the pasta is cooked, drain it and place in a shallow bowl. Spoon the sauce over the pasta, and serve immediately.

*Serves 4*

OTHER PASTA CHOICES: rotini or other curly pasta

# Tahini Rotini with Broccoli and Lemon

Tahini, or sesame paste, is loaded with protein and calcium, while broccoli is a good source of calcium, vitamin C, and other nutrients. It's hard to believe a dish that's so good for you could taste this rich and creamy. Typically used in Middle Eastern cuisine, tahini is available in well-stocked supermarkets, natural foods stores, and at specialty grocers.

2 large garlic cloves, chopped
1 cup cooked chickpeas, drained and rinsed
¼ cup tahini (sesame paste)
Juice and zest of one lemon
2 tablespoons tamari soy sauce
⅛ teaspoon cayenne pepper
1 cup hot vegetable stock or water
1 pound rotini
2 cups broccoli florets
2 tablespoons chopped fresh flat-leaf parsley
2 tablespoons sesame seeds, toasted

In a food processor, combine the garlic, chickpeas, tahini, lemon juice, tamari, and cayenne and process until smooth. Transfer the mixture to a saucepan and stir in the vegetable stock or water. Keep warm over low heat. Cook the rotini in a large pot of salted boiling water, stirring occasionally, until it is al dente, about 8 to 10 minutes. During the last 5 minutes of cooking time, add the broccoli to the pasta. When the pasta is cooked, drain the pasta and broccoli and place in a shallow serving bowl. Add the sauce and toss gently. Sprinkle with the lemon zest, parsley and sesame seeds, and serve immediately.

*Serves 4*

OTHER PASTA CHOICES: fusilli, rotelle

# Fettuccine with Creamy Mushroom and Green Peppercorn Sauce

Bottled green peppercorns packed in brine are available in specialty food stores and well-stocked supermarkets. They have a piquant bite, so alter the amount used according to taste. Mild white mushrooms are preferred in this dish because the flavor of the more assertive wild mushrooms would compete with the flavor of the peppercorns.

2 tablespoons olive oil
3 shallots, chopped
8 ounces white mushrooms, sliced (2½ cups)
2 tablespoons all-purpose flour
2 cups milk or soy milk
1 to 2 teaspoons green peppercorns, drained
Salt
1 pound fettuccine, fresh or dried

Heat the olive oil in a large saucepan over medium heat. Add the shallots and cook for 5 minutes or until softened. Add the mushrooms and cook 2 minutes to soften. Sprinkle the flour over the shallots and mushrooms, and cook, stirring for 1 minute to remove the raw taste from the flour. Reduce heat to low. Slowly add the milk or soy milk, stirring constantly to thicken. Add the peppercorns and salt to taste, and simmer 5 minutes to allow the flavors to blend. Keep warm over very low heat. Cook the fettuccine in a large pot of salted boiling water, stirring occasionally, until it is al dente, 3 to 4 minutes for fresh pasta and about 10 minutes for dried. When the pasta is cooked, drain it and place in a shallow serving bowl. Add the sauce, toss lightly to combine, and serve immediately.

*Serves 4*

OTHER PASTA CHOICES: linguine, perciatelli

# Penne with Artichokes and Oyster Mushrooms

This versatile dish is elegant enough for guests, yet easy enough for a quick weeknight supper. Fresh or frozen artichoke hearts may be used, if you prefer, but avoid the marinated kind as the flavor of the marinade is too strong for this dish.

2 tablespoons olive oil
1 small yellow onion, minced
8 ounces oyster mushrooms, sliced
2 tablespoons all-purpose flour
2 cups soy milk or milk
1 (14-ounce) can artichoke hearts, drained and sliced
1 teaspoon capers, drained
Salt and freshly ground black pepper
1 pound penne

Heat the oil in a large skillet over medium heat. Add the onion and cook until softened, about 5 minutes. Add oyster mushrooms and cook, stirring, for 1 to 2 minutes, or until slightly softened. Stir in the flour and cook 1 minute longer. Slowly stir in the milk or soy milk, stirring constantly until the sauce thickens. Add the artichokes, capers, and salt and pepper to taste. Keep warm over low heat. Cook the penne in a large pot of salted boiling water, stirring occasionally, until it is al dente, about 8 to 10 minutes. When the pasta is cooked, drain it and place in a shallow serving bowl. Add the sauce and toss gently. Serve immediately.

*Serves 4*

OTHER PASTA CHOICES: ziti or other tubular pasta

# Spaghettini with Creamy Garlic-Sage Sauce

The dusky flavor of sage permeates this garlicky sauce. While dried sage could be substituted in a pinch, it's really best to save this recipe for when fresh sage is available. Sage lovers might further embellish this dish with a garnish of crumbled fried sage leaves.

2 tablespoons olive oil
6 garlic cloves, crushed
1 tablespoon chopped fresh sage, or to taste
2 tablespoons all-purpose flour
2 cups soy milk or milk
Salt and freshly ground black pepper
1 pound spaghettini
Freshly shaved Parmesan or grated soy Parmesan cheese

Heat the oil in a large skillet over medium heat. Add the garlic and cook until fragrant and golden brown, being careful not to burn it, about 1 minute. Add the sage and flour, and cook, stirring for 1 minute. Slowly stir in the soy milk or milk, and cook, stirring constantly for 2 minutes to thicken. Season with salt and pepper to taste and keep warm over low heat. Cook the spaghettini in a large pot of salted boiling water, stirring occasionally, until it is al dente, about 2 to 4 minutes. When the pasta is cooked, drain it and place in a large serving bowl. Add the sauce through a fine mesh strainer and toss to combine. Serve immediately, topped with cheese.

*Serves 4*

OTHER PASTA CHOICES: capellini, vermicelli

# Conchiglie and Peas with Red Pepper Coulis

The sweetness of the peas is complemented by the intense flavor of the red pepper coulis. Milk or soy milk is added to the coulis to mellow out the flavor.

1 tablespoon olive oil
1 yellow onion, chopped
4 red bell peppers, diced
2 garlic cloves, chopped
⅓ cup vegetable stock or water
1 teaspoon dried marjoram
Salt and freshly ground black pepper
½ cup milk or soy milk
1 pound conchiglie (small shell pasta)
1 cup frozen peas
2 tablespoons minced fresh basil

Heat the oil in a large skillet over medium heat. Add the onion, bell peppers, and garlic, and cook for 5 minutes to soften, stirring occasionally. Add the stock or water, marjoram, and salt and pepper to taste, cover, and cook 15 minutes longer, or until the vegetables are very soft. Transfer the vegetables to a food processor and puree. With a fine strainer, strain the coulis into a saucepan and stir in the milk. Heat over low heat and keep warm. Cook the conchiglie in a pot of salted boiling water until it is al dente, about 8 minutes. During the last minute of cooking time, add the peas to the pasta. When the pasta is cooked, drain the pasta and peas, and place in a large serving bowl. Add the sauce and combine. Sprinkle with the basil and serve immediately.

*Serves 4*

OTHER PASTA CHOICES: orecchiette, radiatore

# Penne with Vodka-Tomato Sauce

Although the combination may seem unusual, penne with vodka sauce is a popular item on many restaurant menus in Rome. A touch of tarragon is a sweet surprise in this version, and tofu and soy milk stand in for the traditional heavy cream. Adjust the cayenne according to taste. For a smooth sauce, strain it before tossing with the pasta.

1 tablespoon olive oil
1 small yellow onion, chopped
½ cup vodka
1 cup tomato puree
Salt
⅛ teaspoon cayenne pepper, or to taste
¼ cup soft or silken tofu
½ cup soy milk or milk
1 tablespoon fresh minced tarragon, or 1 teaspoon dried
1 teaspoon orange zest
1 pound penne

Heat the oil in a large skillet over medium heat. Add the onion and cook for 5 minutes or until softened. Carefully add the vodka, allowing the alcohol to burn off. Stir in the tomato puree, salt to taste, and the cayenne. Simmer over low heat. Combine the tofu and soy milk in a food processor and puree. Stir the soy mixture into the sauce, add the tarragon and orange zest, and cook over low heat to blend the flavors. Cook the penne in a large pot of salted boiling water, stirring occasionally, until it is al dente, about 8 to 10 minutes. When the pasta is cooked, drain it and place in a shallow serving bowl. Add the sauce, toss to combine, and serve immediately.

*Serves 4*

OTHER PASTA CHOICES: ziti or other tubular pasta

# Linguine with Summer Vegetable Puree

Pureed fresh vegetables combine to create a velvety sauce that tastes like a rich indulgence. Vary the vegetables according to preference and availability.

1 tablespoon olive oil
1 small onion, chopped
1 small red bell pepper, chopped
2 garlic cloves, chopped
1 zucchini, peeled and chopped
1 cup mushrooms, chopped
4 ripe tomatoes, chopped
2 tablespoons tomato paste
Salt and freshly ground black pepper
1 pound linguine
2 tablespoons chopped fresh basil

Heat the oil in a large skillet over medium heat. Add the onion, bell pepper, and garlic, and cook for 5 minutes to soften. Add the zucchini, mushrooms, and tomatoes, and cook 10 to 15 minutes longer, or until the vegetables are very soft. Stir in the tomato paste, and salt and pepper to taste. Transfer the mixture to a food processor and puree. Strain the sauce into a saucepan through a fine mesh strainer, and simmer over low heat for 15 minutes to blend the flavors. Keep warm over low heat, adding a little stock or water if the sauce becomes too thick. Cook the linguine in a large pot of salted boiling water, stirring occasionally, until it is al dente, about 8 to 10 minutes. When the pasta is cooked, drain it and place in a shallow serving bowl. Add the sauce and toss to combine. Sprinkle with the basil and serve immediately.

*Serves 4*

OTHER PASTA CHOICES: fettuccine, pappardelle

# Perciatelli with Brandy-Cashew Cream

This dish tastes as decadent as it sounds, yet it's made with virtuous soy and tasty cashews—both rich in protein and calcium.

¾ cup raw cashews
¼ cup soft or silken tofu
1 cup soy milk or milk
(plus more as needed)
½ teaspoon salt
Cayenne pepper
1 tablespoon olive oil
3 shallots, minced
2 tablespoons brandy
1 pound perciatelli
Minced fresh flat-leaf parsley
Chopped toasted cashews

In a blender, finely grind the cashews. Add the tofu, soy milk or milk, salt, and cayenne to taste, and puree until smooth. Set aside. Heat the oil in a small skillet over medium heat, add the shallots and cook until soft, about 3 minutes. Add the brandy and cook, stirring for 1 minute. Add the shallot mixture to the cashew mixture in the blender and blend well. Transfer to a saucepan and warm over low heat, stirring often. If the sauce is too thick, add more soy milk or milk. Adjust the seasonings. Cook the perciatelli in a large pot of salted boiling water, stirring occasionally, until it is al dente, about 10 minutes. When the pasta is cooked, drain it and place in a serving bowl. Add the sauce and toss to combine. Serve immediately, garnished with the parsley and toasted cashews.

*Serves 4*

OTHER PASTA CHOICES: fettuccine, linguine

# Fettuccine with Sage-Cannellini Puree

Cannellini beans flavored with sage are a popular Tuscan combination. Here the pair is pureed into a creamy pasta sauce enlivened with a splash of balsamic vinegar, a slightly sweet and syrupy aged vinegar from Modena, Italy.

2 tablespoons olive oil
1 small onion, minced
¼ cup fresh sage leaves, minced
1½ cups cooked cannellini beans, drained and rinsed
1 tablespoon balsamic vinegar
½ teaspoon salt
Freshly ground black pepper
⅓ cup hot vegetable stock or water (plus more as needed)
1 pound fettuccine
Whole sage leaves

Heat the oil in a large skillet over medium heat. Add the onion and cook, stirring occasionally, until softened, about 5 minutes. Add the sage and cook 2 minutes. Add the beans, vinegar, salt, and pepper to taste, and stir to blend the flavors. Transfer the bean mixture to a food processor or blender and puree with the vegetable stock or water. Return the sauce to the pan and keep warm over low heat, adding more stock or water if the mixture is too thick. Cook the fettuccine in large pot of salted boiling water, stirring occasionally, until it is al dente, about 10 minutes. When the pasta is cooked, drain it and place in a large shallow bowl. Add the sauce and toss to combine. Serve immediately, garnished with the sage leaves.

*Serves 4*

OTHER PASTA CHOICES: linguine, spaghetti

# ABOUT TOFU AND SOY MILK

Tofu is a cheeselike food made from cooked soybeans. Also known as bean curd, tofu is available in soft, firm, and extra-firm varieties. The texture and taste of tofu can vary greatly from brand to brand, so it is a good idea to experiment until you find the ones you like best. The softer tofu is best for sauces and the firmer tofu works best in sautés and stir-fries.

Fresh organic tofu is available in vacuum-packed tubs in the refrigerator section of natural foods stores and well-stocked supermarkets. Tofu is highly perishable and must be kept refrigerated, so check the expiration date before purchasing. In addition to regular tofu, Japanese-style silken tofu is also available in a variety of textures. Silken tofu can be used to make sauces, puddings, or anything requiring a creamy texture.

Soy milk is a popular nondairy milk made from soybeans that can now be found in most supermarkets and natural foods stores. The flavors and consistencies vary from brand to brand. While some brands of soy milk are found in the refrigerated section and must stay refrigerated even if unopened, most brands are available in aseptic one-quart containers that may be kept unrefrigerated until opened. Soy milk can be substituted in equal measure for cow's milk in recipes.

# Meatless but Meatlike

Thanks to textured vegetable protein (TVP), tempeh, and vegetarian burger crumbles and "sausage," hearty "meat" sauces can be on every vegetarian's menu. Recipes include variations on classics such as carbonara sauce and bolognese sauce as well as a sublime dish redolent of garlic and oyster mushrooms that is reminiscent of white clam sauce.

In addition to meat analogs, many of these recipes call for a variety of flavorful beans to add substance and protein to the meal. Beans have a long and flavorful culinary history in Italian cooking, especially in the southern regions, where chickpeas, lentils, favas, borlotti, and cannellini beans are popular.

Linguine with Red Lentil Sauce (Page 90) and Ziti with Arugula and Fava Beans (page 102) are among the "meaty" offerings that enlist your favorite legumes to help create these wholesome and hearty pasta creations.

Linguine with White "Clam" Sauce

Spaghetti with Vegetarian Bolognese Sauce

Linguine with Red Lentil Sauce

Spaghetti with Carbonara-Style Sauce

Gemelli with Mama's "Meat" Sauce

Fettuccine Cacciatore

Penne with Tomatoes, Chickpeas, and Mint

Tuscan-Style Linguine with Chickpeas, Zucchini, and Rosemary

Tempeh, Mushroom, and Fennel Ragout over Fusilli

Cavatelli with Spicy Veggie Sausage and Tomatoes

Rotini and Cannellini Beans with Roasted Tricolor Peppers

Ziti with Arugula and Fava Beans

Penne and "Sausage" with Kale and Pine Nuts

Pesto-Tossed Fettuccine with White Beans and Sun-Dried Tomatoes

# Linguine with White "Clam" Sauce

Oyster mushrooms, with their slightly briny taste and chewy texture, stand in for the clams in this garlicky sauce. In Italian cooking, grated cheese is not served on pasta dishes containing seafood. Likewise, it is not called for in this vegetarian version.

¼ cup extra-virgin olive oil

3 garlic cloves, finely minced

8 ounces oyster mushrooms, coarsely chopped

⅓ cup dry white wine

½ teaspoon dried basil

¼ teaspoon dried oregano

Salt and freshly ground black pepper

1 teaspoon white miso paste dissolved in ⅓ cup hot water

2 tablespoons minced fresh flat-leaf parsley

1 pound linguine

Heat the oil in a large saucepan over medium heat. Add the garlic and cook until fragrant, about 30 seconds. Add the mushrooms and stir until they begin to soften, about 2 minutes. Stir in the wine, basil, oregano, and salt and pepper to taste, and simmer for about 5 minutes. Stir in the dissolved miso paste and the parsley, and keep warm over low heat. Cook the linguine in a large pot of salted boiling water until it is al dente, about 8 minutes. When the pasta is cooked, drain it and divide among individual plates or shallow bowls. Top with the sauce and serve immediately.

*Serves 4*

OTHER PASTA CHOICES: fettuccine, spaghetti

# Spaghetti with Vegetarian Bolognese Sauce

In Bologna, they serve tagliatelle with their famous meat sauce—elsewhere, spaghetti is the pasta of choice. This vegetarian version uses frozen precooked vegetarian burger crumbles, found in natural foods stores and well-stocked supermarkets, to replace the ground meat. If frozen burger crumbles are unavailable, use one cup TVP (textured vegetable protein) after rehydrating with water or use grated tempeh that has been lightly browned in a skillet.

2 tablespoons olive oil
1 onion, minced
1 stalk celery, minced
1 carrot, minced
2 garlic cloves, minced
¾ cup dry white wine
2 tablespoons tomato paste
1 (28-ounce) can plum tomatoes, finely minced
2½ cups vegetarian burger crumbles, TVP, or tempeh (see note above)
Pinch of nutmeg
½ teaspoon Liquid Smoke (optional)
Salt and freshly ground black pepper
¼ cup soft or silken tofu
¼ cup soy milk or milk
2 tablespoons minced fresh flat-leaf parsley
1 pound spaghetti
Freshly grated Parmesan or soy Parmesan cheese

Heat the oil in a large skillet over medium heat. Add the onion, celery, carrot, and garlic. Cover and cook until soft, about 10 minutes. Remove cover, stir in the wine, and simmer for 5 minutes to reduce the liquid. Add the tomato paste, tomatoes, vegetarian burger, nutmeg, Liquid Smoke if you are using it, and salt and pepper to taste, and simmer over low heat for 10 minutes. Meanwhile, combine the tofu and soy milk or milk in a blender and blend until smooth. Stir the tofu mixture and the parsley into the sauce and keep it warm over low heat. Cook the spaghetti in a large pot of salted boiling water, stirring occasionally, until it is al dente, about 8 minutes. When the pasta is cooked, drain it and place in a large serving bowl. Add the sauce and toss gently. Serve immediately, passing a bowl of cheese at the table.

*Serves 4*

OTHER PASTA CHOICES: linguine, fettuccine

# Linguine with Red Lentil Sauce

Although lentils are more prominent in Indian and Middle Eastern cooking, they are also used in Italian cuisine. This thin lens-shaped legume is rich in protein, calcium, iron, and B complex vitamins. Since lentils do not require soaking and cook up quickly, this recipe doesn't require a lot of advance planning to get dinner on the table.

¾ cup dried red lentils, sorted and rinsed
2 carrots, cut diagonally in ¼-inch slices
1 stalk celery, diced
3 tablespoons olive oil
1 garlic clove, minced
1 (6-ounce) can tomato paste
Salt and freshly ground black pepper
1 pound linguine
2 tablespoons chopped fresh flat-leaf parsley

Place the lentils, carrots, and celery in a pot of salted boiling water. Reduce heat to medium-low and simmer until tender, about 30 minutes. Drain the vegetables, reserving 2 cups of the cooking liquid. Toss the lentil mixture with 1 tablespoon of the oil and set aside. Heat the remaining 2 tablespoons of oil in a large skillet over medium heat. Add the garlic and cook until fragrant, about 30 seconds. Stir in the tomato paste and cook for 2 minutes to mellow the flavor of the paste. Stir in the lentil cooking liquid, blending until smooth. Add the lentil mixture, and salt and pepper to taste. Simmer over low heat to blend the flavors. If the liquid evaporates, add some water. Cook the linguine in a large pot of salted boiling water, stirring occasionally, until it is al dente, about 8 minutes. When the pasta is cooked, drain it and divide among individual plates or shallow bowls. Top with the sauce, sprinkle with parsley, and serve immediately.

*Serves 4*

OTHER PASTA CHOICES: fettuccine, pappardelle

# Spaghetti with Carbonara-Style Sauce

This health-conscious interpretation of carbonara sauce—the original calls for bacon and eggs—can employ either tempeh bacon or vegetarian Canadian bacon to stand in for the Italian pancetta. Vegetarian bacon products are available at well-stocked supermarkets and natural foods stores.

2 tablespoons olive oil
4 ounces tempeh bacon or vegetarian Canadian bacon, chopped
½ cup soft or silken tofu
½ cup grated Parmesan or soy Parmesan cheese
1 cup milk or soy milk
Salt and freshly ground black pepper
1 pound spaghetti

Heat the oil in a large skillet over medium heat. Add the vegetarian bacon and cook, stirring frequently, until lightly browned, about 5 minutes. Set aside. In a blender combine the tofu with ¼ cup of the cheese, the milk or soy milk, and salt and pepper to taste. Set aside. Cook the spaghetti in a large pot of salted boiling water, stirring occasionally, until it is al dente, about 8 minutes. When the pasta is cooked, drain it and place in a shallow serving bowl. Add the tofu mixture, the remaining ¼ cup cheese, and all but 2 tablespoons of the vegetarian bacon, and toss to combine. Top with several grindings of black pepper and the remaining vegetarian bacon, and serve immediately.

*Serves 4*

OTHER PASTA CHOICES: fusilli, perciatelli

# Gemelli with Mama's "Meat"

Frozen vegetarian burger crumbles are a boon to meatless cooking. Precooked and ready to use, they can be used in any recipe calling for cooked ground beef.

1 tablespoon olive oil
1 onion, minced
1 carrot, diced
2 large garlic cloves, minced
1 (6-ounce) can tomato paste
1 (28-ounce) can crushed Italian plum tomatoes
1½ cups vegetable stock or water
¼ cup minced fresh flat-leaf parsley
1 teaspoon dried basil
½ teaspoon dried oregano
Salt and freshly ground black pepper
1 (12-ounce) package vegetarian burger crumbles
1 pound gemelli
Freshly grated Parmesan or soy Parmesan cheese

Heat the oil in a large skillet over medium heat. Add the onion, carrot, and garlic. Cover and cook for 5 minutes or until the vegetables soften. Add the tomato paste, stirring to blend. Add the tomatoes, vegetable stock or water, parsley, basil, oregano, and salt and pepper to taste. Simmer for 30 minutes, stirring occasionally. Add the vegetarian burger and cook 15 minutes longer to blend flavors. Cook the gemelli in a large pot of salted boiling water, stirring occasionally, until it is al dente, about 8 to 10 minutes. When the pasta is cooked, drain it, place in a serving bowl, and top with the sauce. Sprinkle with grated cheese and serve immediately, with extra cheese to pass at the table.

*Serves 4*

OTHER PASTA CHOICES: **cavatappi, fusilli**

# Fettuccine Cacciatore

When my mom made chicken cacciatore, I'd skip the chicken and enjoy the vegetables and pappardelle that went with it. Here, I've reinvented her recipe using tempeh and fettuccine.

2 tablespoons olive oil
8 ounces tempeh, cut into 1-inch pieces
½ cup dry white wine
1 stalk celery, coarsely chopped
1 carrot, coarsely chopped
1 green bell pepper, coarsely chopped
1 garlic clove, minced
1 (28-ounce) can diced tomatoes
1 teaspoon minced fresh rosemary, or ½ teaspoon dried
1 teaspoon minced fresh marjoram, or ½ teaspoon dried
Salt and freshly ground black pepper
1 pound fettuccine

Heat 1 tablespoon of the oil in a skillet over medium heat. Add the tempeh and cook until lightly browned, about 5 minutes. Remove the tempeh from the skillet and set aside. Deglaze the pan with the wine, stirring to scrape up any browned bits. Reduce the wine by half and set aside. Heat the remaining oil in a large saucepan over medium heat. Add the celery, carrot, bell pepper, and garlic. Cover and cook until soft, about 10 minutes. Remove cover, add the tomatoes, rosemary, and marjoram, and season with salt and pepper to taste. Simmer the sauce for 10 minutes, then add the tempeh and wine, and simmer 20 minutes longer. Keep warm over low heat. Cook the fettuccine in a large pot of salted boiling water, stirring occasionally, until it is al dente, about 10 minutes. When the pasta is cooked, drain it and place in a serving bowl. Top with the sauce and serve immediately.

*Serves 4*

OTHER PASTA CHOICES: pappardelle, linguine

# Penne with Tomatoes, Chickpeas, and Mint

Meaty chickpeas provide substance to this dish, which is best made in the summer when fresh ripe tomatoes and mint are at their peak. While mint is more commonly thought of as an ingredient in Greek and Middle Eastern cooking, it is favored by Italian cooks as well.

¼ cup olive oil
2 shallots, minced
3 to 4 large ripe tomatoes, chopped
1½ cups cooked chickpeas, drained and rinsed
1 bunch scallions, minced
Salt and freshly ground black pepper
1 pound penne
¼ cup minced fresh mint

Heat the oil in a large skillet over medium heat. Add the shallots and cook until softened, about 5 minutes. Add the tomatoes, chickpeas, scallions, and salt and pepper to taste. Simmer until heated through, about 5 minutes. Keep warm over low heat. Cook the penne in a large pot of boiling water, stirring occasionally, until it is al dente, about 8 to 10 minutes. When the pasta is cooked, drain it and place in a large serving bowl. Add the tomato and chickpea mixture and the mint, and toss gently to combine. Serve immediately.

*Serves 4*

OTHER PASTA CHOICES: ziti or other tubular pasta

# Tuscan-Style Linguine with Chickpeas, Zucchini, and Rosemary

Beans are so prevalent in Tuscan cooking that the people of Tuscany are called "bean eaters." For variety, fresh basil or another fragrant herb may be substituted for the rosemary.

2 small zucchini, halved lengthwise
2 tablespoons olive oil
2 garlic cloves, minced
2 tablespoons chopped fresh rosemary leaves, or to taste
1 (15-ounce) can Italian plum tomatoes, chopped
1½ cups cooked chickpeas, drained and rinsed
¼ teaspoon hot red pepper flakes
Salt and freshly ground black pepper
1 pound linguine
Freshly shaved Parmesan or soy Parmesan cheese

Cut the zucchini into ¼-inch slices. Heat the oil in a large saucepan over medium heat. Add the zucchini and cook until slightly soft, about 2 minutes. Add the garlic and cook until fragrant, about 30 seconds. Stir in the rosemary, tomatoes, chickpeas, red pepper flakes, and salt and pepper to taste. Cook, stirring occasionally, for 10 minutes to blend the flavors. Cook the linguine in a large pot of salted boiling water, stirring occasionally, until it is al dente, about 8 minutes. When the pasta is cooked, drain it and place in a large shallow bowl. Add the sauce and toss gently to combine. Serve immediately, passing the cheese at the table.

*Serves 4*

OTHER PASTA CHOICES: fettuccine, spaghetti

# Tempeh, Mushroom, and Fennel Ragout over Fusilli

This warming ragout tastes even better the day after it's prepared. Consider making it ahead to enjoy its fullest flavor. Tempeh is made from compressed soybeans that are formed into cakes. It is available in the refrigerated case of natural foods stores and some supermarkets.

2 tablespoons olive oil
8 ounces tempeh, chopped
1 small yellow onion, chopped
1 fennel bulb, chopped
8 ounces white mushrooms, sliced (2½ cups)
½ cup dry white wine
1 (29-ounce) can Italian plum tomatoes, chopped
1 bay leaf
1 cup vegetable stock or water
1 teaspoon dried basil
½ teaspoon dried oregano
½ teaspoon salt
⅛ teaspoon freshly ground black pepper
1 pound fusilli
Freshly grated Pecorino Romano or soy Parmesan cheese

Heat 1 tablespoon of the oil in large skillet over medium heat. Add the tempeh and cook until golden brown, about 5 minutes. Remove the tempeh from the skillet and set aside. Add the remaining 1 tablespoon of oil and reheat the skillet. Add the onion and fennel, and cook until the vegetables are soft, about 10 minutes. Stir in the mushrooms. Add the wine and cook until the alcohol cooks off, about 2 minutes. Stir in the tomatoes, the reserved tempeh, bay leaf, vegetable stock or water, basil, oregano, salt, and pepper, and bring to a boil. Reduce heat to low and simmer, stirring occasionally, until the liquid reduces and the flavors have developed, about 20 minutes. Discard the bay leaf. Cook the fusilli in a large pot of salted boiling water, stirring occasionally, until it is al dente, about 8 to 10 minutes. When the pasta is cooked, drain it and divide the pasta among individual plates or shallow bowls. Top with the sauce and serve immediately, passing cheese at the table.

*Serves 4*

OTHER PASTA CHOICES: gemelli, cavatappi

# Cavatelli with Spicy Veggie Sausage and Tomatoes

There are a variety of vegetarian sausages on the market, however, most are not very spicy and need a little encouragement from your spice cupboard. If veggie sausage is unavailable, use ground veggie burgers or another ground meat alternative and increase the spices to give it a "sausage" flavor.

2 tablespoons olive oil
1 carrot, finely chopped
1 onion, finely chopped
1 clove garlic, minced
2 tablespoons tomato paste
1 tablespoon minced fresh marjoram, or 1 teaspoon dried
1 teaspoon ground fennel seed
1 (29-ounce) can Italian plum tomatoes, chopped
½ teaspoon salt
⅛ teaspoon freshly ground pepper
⅛ teaspoon cayenne pepper, or to taste
8 ounces cooked vegetarian sausage, crumbled
Hot red pepper flakes
1 pound frozen cavatelli
Freshly shaved Parmesan or grated soy Parmesan cheese
Minced fresh flat-leaf parsley

In a large saucepan, heat 1 tablespoon of the oil over medium heat. Add the carrot, onion, and garlic, and cook until soft, about 5 to 7 minutes. Stir in the tomato paste, marjoram, ground fennel, and the tomatoes. Season with the salt, pepper, and cayenne, and simmer about 20 minutes.  Stir in the sausage and red pepper flakes to taste, and simmer 5 minutes longer to blend the flavors. Keep warm over low heat. Cook the cavatelli in a large pot of salted boiling water, stirring occasionally, until it is tender but still chewy, about 8 minutes. When the pasta is cooked, drain it and divide among individual plates or shallow bowls. Top with the sauce, a few shavings of Parmesan, and a sprinkling of parsley. Serve immediately, passing additional cheese at the table.

*Serves 4*

OTHER PASTA CHOICES: farfalle, gemelli

# Rotini and Cannellini Beans with Roasted Tricolor Peppers

Use tricolor rotini with the tricolored peppers for a striking presentation. The creamy white cannellini beans, sometimes called white kidney beans, add protein and texture to this colorful dish.

1 red bell pepper
1 green bell pepper
1 yellow bell pepper
2 tablespoons olive oil
1 garlic clove, minced
1½ cups cooked cannellini beans, drained and rinsed
¼ cup vegetable stock or water
2 tablespoons minced fresh flat-leaf parsley
1 tablespoon minced fresh basil, or 1 teaspoon dried
½ teaspoon minced fresh oregano, or ¼ teaspoon dried
1 pound rotini, tricolor if possible
Salt and freshly ground black pepper
Freshly grated Parmesan or soy Parmesan cheese

Preheat the broiler.

Halve the bell peppers lengthwise, remove the stems and seeds, and place on a broiler rack, cut side down. Broil until the skin blackens and blisters, 5 to 10 minutes, then remove the peppers from the oven and place in a paper or plastic bag. Close tightly and set aside for 10 minutes. Remove the peppers from the bag and scrape off the charred skins. Cut the peppers into ¼-inch strips. Heat the oil in a large skillet over medium heat. Add the garlic and cook until fragrant, about 30 seconds. Add the peppers and cook 2 to 3 minutes to blend the flavors. Stir in the beans, vegetable stock or water, parsley, basil, and oregano, and cook until heated through, about 5 minutes. Cook the rotini in a large pot of salted boiling water, stirring occasionally, until it is al dente, about 8 to 10 minutes. When the pasta is cooked, drain it and place in a shallow serving bowl. Add the pepper mixture, season to taste with salt and pepper, and toss gently to combine. Serve immediately, passing cheese at the table.

*Serves 4*

OTHER PASTA CHOICES: rotelle, fusilli

# Ziti with Arugula and Fava Beans

The peppery flavor of the arugula provides the perfect complement to the mellow fava beans. Fresh favas can be difficult to find but well worth it when you do. You will need to peel the tough skin from the favas before cooking, unless you're lucky enough to find the highly prized tender young beans.

1 cup peeled fava beans
2 tablespoons olive oil
1 garlic clove, sliced paper thin
1 bunch arugula, trimmed
½ cup vegetable stock or water
Salt and freshly ground black pepper
1 pound ziti
1 tablespoon minced fresh flat-leaf parsley
Freshly grated Pecorino Romano or soy Parmesan cheese

Cook the fava beans in boiling water until just tender, about 5 to 7 minutes. Drain and set aside. Heat the oil in a large skillet over medium heat. Add the garlic, arugula, and vegetable stock or water, and cook, stirring until the arugula is wilted, about 2 minutes. Add the beans, season with salt and pepper to taste, and keep warm over low heat. Cook the ziti in large pot of salted boiling water, stirring occasionally, until it is al dente, about 8 to 10 minutes. When the pasta is cooked, drain it and place in a large serving bowl. Add the arugula and bean mixture and parsley, and toss gently to combine. Serve immediately, passing grated cheese at the table.

*Serves 4*

OTHER PASTA CHOICES: penne, mostaccioli

# Penne and "Sausage" with Kale and Pine Nuts

This hearty one-dish meal is a great way to get picky eaters to enjoy their greens—the chopped kale takes on the flavor of the spicy veggie sausage, and the pine nuts add a mellow crunch. Spinach can be substituted for the kale, if you prefer.

2 tablespoons olive oil
1 garlic clove, minced
About 4 ounces kale, coarsely chopped (3 cups)
1 cup vegetable stock or water
8 ounces vegetarian sausage links, cut into 1-inch pieces
Hot red pepper flakes
Salt and freshly ground black pepper
1 pound penne
¼ cup toasted pine nuts

Heat 1 tablespoon of the oil in a large skillet. Add the garlic and cook until fragrant, about 30 seconds. Add the kale and vegetable stock or water, and cook until the kale is tender, about 10 minutes. Set aside. In a medium skillet, heat the remaining 1 tablespoon of oil over medium heat. Add the vegetarian sausage and cook until lightly browned all over, about 5 minutes. Add the sausage to the kale along with red pepper flakes to taste. Season with salt and pepper to taste, and return the mixture to the burner over low heat to blend the flavors and heat through. Cook the penne in a large pot of salted boiling water, stirring occasionally, until just tender, about 10 minutes. When the pasta is cooked, drain it and place in a shallow serving bowl. Add the sausage and kale mixture, and toss gently to combine. Divide among individual plates and top with the pine nuts. Serve immediately.

*Serves 4*

OTHER PASTA CHOICES: farfalle, cavatappi

# Pesto-Tossed Fettuccine with White Beans and Sun-Dried Tomatoes

I like to make this dish during the winter using pesto that I have stashed in the freezer from the previous summer. Note: Commercially prepared pesto is available in supermarkets and specialty grocers. If you prefer to make your own, use the pesto recipe on page 14.

2 tablespoons olive oil
¼ cup chopped shallots
1 clove garlic, minced
¼ cup oil-packed sun-dried tomatoes
1½ cups cooked cannellini beans, drained and rinsed
Hot red pepper flakes
Salt and freshly ground black pepper
1 pound fettuccine
⅓ cup basil pesto (page 14)

Heat the oil in a large skillet over medium heat. Add the shallots and garlic, and cook until softened, about 3 minutes. Cut the tomatoes into thin strips and add to the skillet, along with the beans, and red pepper flakes, salt, and pepper to taste. Keep warm over low heat. Cook the fettuccine in a large pot of salted boiling water, stirring occasionally, until it is al dente, about 10 minutes. When the pasta is cooked, drain it and place in a shallow serving bowl. Add the pesto and toss to coat the pasta. Add the bean mixture and toss gently to combine. Serve immediately.

*Serves 4*

OTHER PASTA CHOICES: linguine, spaghetti

# ABOUT TEMPEH AND TVP

Tempeh is a protein-rich meat alternative made from fermented, compressed soybeans. It has a distinctive nutty flavor, meaty texture, and the ability to take on surrounding flavors. Tempeh can be made solely from soy but is also available with one or more grains blended into it. Tempeh keeps well both refrigerated and frozen and can be found in natural foods stores and some supermarkets.

TVP is an economical dehydrated meat alternative made from compressed soy flour. Virtually flavorless, TVP granules reconstitute with hot water or other liquid and nearly double in volume, a fact to be aware of when using it in recipes. Like tofu and tempeh, TVP readily absorbs the flavors of surrounding ingredients. With its chewy texture and ground meat-like appearance, TVP makes a great addition to pasta sauces. TVP is often available in the bulk food bins at natural foods stores and some supermarkets.

A convenient ready-to-use alternative to dehydrated TVP granules are the frozen vegetarian burger crumbles also found in natural foods stores and many supermarkets. Made from soy protein and whole grain, these products are precooked and can be substituted in equal measure for cooked ground beef.

# Stuffed, Layered, Baked

This chapter features several variations on the ever-popular baked pasta dish—lasagne. From the Latin *laganum,* lasagne had its origins in ancient Rome, where strips of dough were baked together with other ingredients. (Note: lasagn*e* refers to the dish; lasagn*a* refers to the noodle.)

In addition to lasagne, this chapter includes great ways to prepare stuffed shells, manicotti, ravioli, and other baked or stuffed creations. Many of these dishes are well suited to feed a crowd and can be made ahead and popped in the oven at dinnertime.

Main dish casseroles such as Southwestern Pasta Gratin (page 119) and Tetrazzini-Style Fettuccine (page 130) are destined to become family favorites, while Tomato-Basil Pasta Spirals (page 120) and Lemony Chard-Stuffed Shells (page 128) make an impressive treat for guests. Also in this chapter is an amazingly healthful and delicious version of that popular comfort food: macaroni and cheese.

Eggplant Parmigiana Lasagne

Pesto Lasagne Bandiera

Autumn Harvest Lasagne

Tofu Ravioli with Baby Spinach and Pine Nuts

Florentine-Style Tofu Manicotti

"Sausage" and Fennel Cannelloni

Enlightened Macaroni and Cheese

Southwestern Pasta Gratin

Tomato-Basil Pasta Spirals

Vegetable Pastitsio

Baked Penne with Broccoli and Tofu

Pasta-Stuffed Peppers

Lemony Chard-Stuffed Shells

Spinach Tortellini with Peas and Hazelnut Gremolata

Tetrazzini-Style Fettuccine

# Eggplant Parmigiana Lasagne

Two favorites—lasagne and eggplant parmigiana are combined in one delicious dish. What could be better? You can use a good-quality bottled pasta sauce or make your own using the recipe on page 66. Instead of the regular lasagna noodles, you may substitute the ones that do not require precooking.

2 tablespoons olive oil
1 eggplant, cut into ¼-inch slices
1 pound lasagna noodles
1 pound firm tofu, drained and patted dry
½ cup freshly grated Parmesan or soy Parmesan cheese
3 tablespoons minced fresh flat-leaf parsley
Salt and freshly ground black pepper
3 cups tomato-based pasta sauce, bottled or homemade
1 cup shredded mozzarella or soy mozzarella cheese

Preheat the oven to 350°F. Heat the oil in a large skillet over medium heat, add the eggplant, and cook until lightly browned on both sides, about 5 minutes, cooking in batches if necessary. Transfer the eggplant to a large plate lined with paper towels and set aside. Cook the lasagna noodles according to the package directions. While the pasta is cooking, crumble the tofu into a large bowl. Add ¼ cup of the Parmesan, parsley, and salt and pepper to taste, and mix well. Spread a layer of the pasta sauce in the bottom of a 9-by-13-inch baking dish. Top the sauce with a layer of noodles. Top the noodles with half of the eggplant, then spread half the tofu mixture over the eggplant. Repeat with another layer of noodles, and top with more sauce. Repeat the layering process with the remaining eggplant mixture and the remaining tofu mixture, ending with a layer of noodles topped with sauce. Sprinkle the mozzarella and the remaining Parmesan on top. Bake for 40 minutes. Remove from the oven and let stand for 10 minutes before cutting.

*Serves 8*

# Pesto Lasagne Bandiera

*Bandiera* means "flag" and this lasagne is so named because its components are red, white, and green—the colors of the Italian flag. If you use bottled pasta sauce and no-boil lasagna noodles, it will cut the preparation time in half. If you use homemade pasta sauce, the recipe on page 51 is a good choice.

*For the pesto:*

    2 garlic cloves

    ¼ cup pine nuts

    1½ cups fresh basil leaves, packed

    ¼ teaspoon salt

    ⅓ cup extra-virgin olive oil

    ¼ cup grated Parmesan or soy Parmesan cheese

*For the lasagne:*

    1 pound lasagna noodles

    1 pound firm tofu, drained

    12 ounces soft or silken tofu

    1 cup pesto

    Salt and freshly ground black pepper

    3 cups tomato-based pasta sauce, bottled or homemade

    1 cup grated mozzarella or soy mozzarella cheese

    2 tablespoons minced fresh flat-leaf parsley

*To make the pesto:* Place the garlic and pine nuts in a food processor and pulse until coarsely chopped. Add the basil leaves and salt and pepper to taste, and blend thoroughly to a paste, scraping down the sides of the bowl as necessary. With the machine running, slowly pour the olive oil through the feed tube and process until well blended. Transfer to a small bowl and stir in the Parmesan.

*Makes 1 cup*

*To prepare the lasagne:* Cook the lasagna noodles according to the package directions. Preheat the oven to 350°F.

Crumble the firm tofu into a large bowl. Add the soft tofu and pesto, and mix until well combined. Season with salt and pepper to taste. Spoon a layer of the pasta sauce into the bottom of 9-by-13-inch baking dish. Top with a layer of noodles. Spread half of the tofu mixture evenly over the noodles. Repeat with another layer of noodles, sauce, and the remaining tofu mixture. Finish with a final layer of noodles and sauce, and top with the cheese. Cover with foil and bake for 25 minutes. Uncover and bake 10 minutes longer. Remove from the oven and let stand for 10 minutes before cutting. Garnish with parsley and serve.

*Serves 8*

# *Autumn Harvest Lasagne*

Wild mushrooms, butternut squash, and pecans make this out-of-the-ordinary lasagne extraordinary. Serve with steamed broccoli or another green vegetable.

1 tablespoon olive oil
1 onion, minced
1 pound butternut squash, peeled and coarsely grated
1 garlic clove, minced
8 ounces porcini mushrooms, sliced
1 teaspoon dried thyme
Salt and freshly ground black pepper
1 pound lasagna noodles
1 pound soft tofu
1 cup soy milk or milk
½ cup chopped pecans, toasted
¼ cup minced fresh flat-leaf parsley
1 cup shredded mozzarella or soy mozzarella cheese

Preheat oven to 375°F.

Heat the oil in a saucepan over medium heat. Add the onion, squash, and garlic, and cover and cook for 10 minutes, or until soft. Add the mushrooms, thyme, and salt and pepper to taste. Cook for 5 minutes. Transfer to a bowl and set aside. Cook the lasagna noodles according to the package directions. Combine the tofu, soy milk, and salt to taste in a food processor and process until well blended. Spread a thin layer of the tofu mixture in the bottom of a 9-by-13-inch baking dish. Arrange a layer of the noodles on top of the tofu mixture, and top with half of the squash mixture. Sprinkle with half of the pecans. Top with layers of the remaining squash, noodles, and tofu. Top with the cheese and the remaining pecans, and bake for 30 minutes. Remove from the oven and let stand for 5 minutes before cutting.

*Serves 8*

# Tofu Ravioli with Baby Spinach and Pine Nuts

Frozen tofu ravioli are available in natural foods stores, but cheese ravioli, available in most supermarkets, may be substituted. Tender baby spinach, once only found in costly salad blends, is showing up in supermarket produce sections, where it is available loose for customers to bag as much as they want.

1 pound frozen tofu ravioli
2 tablespoons extra-virgin olive oil
2 shallots, minced
4 cups fresh baby spinach
Salt and freshly ground black pepper
2 tablespoons pine nuts, toasted

Drop the ravioli into a large pot of salted boiling water a few at a time. Cook according to the package directions. While the ravioli are cooking, heat 1 tablespoon of the oil in a large skillet over medium heat. Add the shallots and cook until soft, about 4 minutes. Add the spinach and cook until wilted, about 2 minutes. Add the remaining oil, season with salt and pepper to taste, and set aside. When the pasta is cooked, drain it and divide among individual plates. Top with the spinach mixture and pine nuts. Serve immediately.

*Serves 4 to 6*

# Florentine-Style Tofu Manicotti

This lovely dish is a good choice to prepare in advance for a dinner party for a no-fuss entree that you can just pop into the oven when needed. With soy milk and two kinds of tofu, it's a delicious way to enjoy good-for-you soy.

12 manicotti tubes
3 tablespoons olive oil
2 scallions, minced
2 (10-ounce) packages frozen chopped spinach, thawed
¼ teaspoon ground nutmeg
Salt and freshly ground black pepper
1 pound firm tofu, drained and crumbled
12 ounces soft or silken tofu
2 cups soy milk or milk
1 cup fresh breadcrumbs
1 cup grated mozzarella or soy mozzarella cheese

Cook the manicotti in a large pot of salted boiling water, stirring occasionally, until it is al dente, about 8 minutes. When the pasta is cooked, drain it and run it under cold water. Set aside. Heat 1 tablespoon of the oil in a skillet over medium heat. Add the scallions and cook until softened, about 5 minutes. Squeeze the spinach to remove as much liquid as possible and add to the skillet. Season with nutmeg and salt and pepper to taste, and cook 2 minutes, stirring to blend the flavors. Transfer the spinach mixture to a large bowl, add the firm tofu, and stir to blend well. Set aside.

Preheat the oven to 350°F. Lightly oil a 9-by-13-inch baking dish.

In a blender or food processor, combine the soft or silken tofu with the soy milk and salt and pepper to taste. Spread a layer of the tofu sauce on the bottom of the prepared dish. Using a teaspoon, place the spinach stuffing in the manicotti tubes. Arrange the stuffed manicotti in single layer in the baking dish. Spoon the remaining sauce over the manicotti. In a small bowl, mix the breadcrumbs and remaining 2 tablespoons of oil with a fork, and sprinkle over the manicotti. Top with the cheese and cover the dish with foil. Bake for 20 minutes. Uncover, and bake 10 minutes longer to allow the top to become golden brown.

*Serves 4*

OTHER PASTA CHOICES: cannelloni, large shells

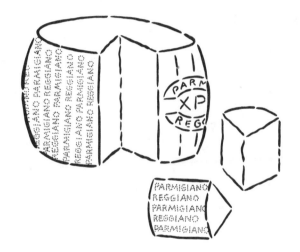

# "Sausage" and Fennel Cannelloni

Although cannelloni is virtually indistinguishable from manicotti, the difference usually lies in the filling. Manicotti usually contains a cheese filling, and cannelloni is usually made with a meaty filling.

12 cannelloni tubes
2 fennel bulbs, coarsely chopped
1 tablespoon olive oil
1 small yellow onion, minced
1 (15-ounce) can tomatoes, chopped
12 ounces cooked vegetarian sausage, crumbled
½ teaspoon hot red pepper flakes
½ teaspoon dried oregano
½ teaspoon dried basil
Salt and freshly ground black pepper
1 cup fresh breadcrumbs
1 cup grated mozzarella or soy mozzarella cheese
3 cups tomato-based pasta sauce, bottled or homemade (page 66)

Cook the cannelloni in a large pot of salted boiling water, stirring occasionally, until it is al dente, about 8 minutes. When the pasta is cooked, drain it and run it under cold water. Set aside. Lightly steam the fennel until tender, about 5 minutes. Set aside. Heat the oil in a large skillet over medium heat. Add the onion and cook until softened, about 5 minutes. Add the tomatoes, the vegetarian sausage, red pepper flakes, oregano, basil, and salt and pepper to taste, and cook 10 minutes, stirring to blend the flavors. Transfer the sausage mixture to a large bowl, and add the breadcrumbs and half the cheese, stirring to blend well. Set aside.

Preheat the oven to 350°F. Lightly oil a 9-by-13-inch baking dish.

Spread a layer of the pasta sauce on the bottom of the prepared dish. Using a teaspoon, place the sausage stuffing in the cannelloni, arranging the stuffed tubes in a single layer in the baking dish. Spoon the remaining sauce over the cannelloni, top with the remaining cheese, and cover with foil. Bake for 20 minutes. Uncover, and bake 10 minutes longer to allow the tops to become golden brown.

*Serves 4*

OTHER PASTA CHOICES: manicotti, large shells

# Enlightened Macaroni
# and Cheese

Besides delivering the health benefits of soy, tofu and soy milk significantly reduce the fat, calories, and cholesterol  in this healthful macaroni and cheese.

    1 tablespoon olive oil
    1 yellow onion, minced
    8 ounces soft or silken tofu, drained
    2 cups soy milk or milk
    Dash of Tabasco sauce
    ¾ teaspoon salt
    ⅛ teaspoon freshly ground black pepper
    Pinch of nutmeg
    12 ounces elbow macaroni
    1 cup grated cheddar or soy cheddar cheese
    ½ cup dry breadcrumbs
    Paprika

Preheat the oven to 375°F. Lightly oil a 3-quart baking dish. Heat the oil in a small skillet over medium heat, add the onion, cover, and cook until soft, about 5 to 7 minutes. Set aside. In a blender, combine the tofu, soy milk, Tabasco, salt, pepper, nutmeg, and the reserved onion, and blend until smooth. Cook the macaroni in a large pot of salted boiling water until just tender but still firm, about 8 minutes. When the pasta is cooked, drain it and place in a large bowl. Add the sauce and half of the cheese, and stir until well combined. Spoon into the prepared dish and top with the breadcrumbs and the remaining cheese, and sprinkle with paprika. Cover and bake for 20 minutes. Uncover and bake 10 minutes longer to lightly brown the top.

*Serves 6*

OTHER PASTA CHOICES:  small shells, rotini

# Southwestern Pasta Gratin

Similar to macaroni and cheese, this family favorite has a taste of the Southwest thanks to picante sauce, chiles, and other spicy ingredients. All you need is a green salad to complete the meal.

8 ounces elbow macaroni
1 tablespoon olive oil
2 garlic cloves, minced
1 jalapeño chile, seeded and minced
1½ cups cooked pinto beans, drained and rinsed
1 tablespoon chili powder, or more to taste
½ teaspoon dried oregano
1½ cups bottled picante sauce
1 (14-ounce) can diced tomatoes
Salt and freshly ground black pepper
1 cup shredded cheddar or soy cheddar cheese

Cook the macaroni in a large pot of salted boiling water, stirring occasionally, until it is al dente, about 8 minutes. When the pasta is cooked, drain it and set aside.

Preheat the oven to 350°F. Lightly oil a 2½-quart baking dish.

Heat the oil in a large skillet over low heat, add the garlic and jalapeño, and cook until softened, about 1 minute. Add the beans, chili powder, and oregano. Stir in the picante sauce and tomatoes, and mix well. Reduce heat to low and simmer for 5 minutes. Season with salt and pepper to taste. In a large bowl, combine the macaroni with the bean and tomato mixture and transfer to the prepared dish. Top with the cheese. Cover and bake for 25 minutes. Uncover and continue baking 5 to 10 minutes longer or until the top is lightly browned.

*Serves 4*

OTHER PASTA CHOICES: small shells, rotelle

# Tomato-Basil Pasta Spirals

Use lasagna noodles to create pasta spirals for a lovely presentation. I like to serve them with roasted pencil-thin asparagus and a wedge of warm focaccia bread. A light fruity barolo is a good wine choice.

2 tablespoons olive oil

4 shallots, minced

2 tablespoons tomato paste

¼ cup dry red wine

1 (16-ounce) can Italian plum tomatoes, finely chopped

Salt and freshly ground black pepper

¼ cup minced fresh basil

12 lasagna noodles

1 garlic clove, minced

1 pound firm tofu, drained and crumbled

3 oil-packed sun-dried tomatoes, chopped

¼ cup pesto (page 110)

⅓ cup fresh breadcrumbs

1 teaspoon salt

⅛ teaspoon cayenne pepper

Whole basil leaves

Heat 1 tablespoon of the oil in a saucepan over medium-low heat. Add half the shallots and cook 5 minutes, stirring frequently. Stir in the tomato paste, then add the wine, tomatoes, and salt and pepper to taste. Simmer for 10 minutes, stir in the minced basil, and keep warm over low heat. Cook the noodles in a large pot of salted boiling water, stirring occasionally, until they are al dente, about 8 minutes. When the noodles are cooked, drain them, lay them flat on a work surface, and pat dry. Heat the remaining oil in a small skillet over medium heat, add the remaining shallots and the garlic, and cook until soft, about 5 minutes. Transfer the mixture to a food processor and add the tofu, sun-dried tomatoes, pesto, breadcrumbs, salt, and cayenne. Process until well blended. Transfer the mixture to a bowl and refrigerate for 30 minutes.

Preheat the oven to 350°F. Lightly oil a shallow 9-by-13-inch baking pan.

Divide the filling equally among the noodles, spreading it onto the surface of each noodle. Roll up each noodle tightly into a spiral-shaped roll. Place the pasta spirals seam-side down on the prepared pan. Lightly nap the spirals with 1 cup of the sauce. Cover the pan with foil and bake for 20 minutes or until hot. Spread a small amount of sauce on each plate, remove the spirals from the pan, and stand them upright on top of the sauce. Spoon the remaining sauce over the pasta spirals and garnish with whole basil leaves.

*Serves 4 to 6*

# Vegetable Pastitsio

Based on the classic Greek pasta dish that is usually made with ground beef and lamb, I think this vegetarian version is as rich and satisfying as the original. It's an ideal party food because you can assemble it ahead and bake it just before serving. To further the no-fuss theme, I like to serve it with marinated green beans and cherry tomatoes with toasted pine nuts, which I also prepare in advance.

12 ounces elbow macaroni
1 tablespoon olive oil
1 onion, chopped
2 garlic cloves, chopped
1 pound vegetarian burger crumbles
½ teaspoon dried oregano
½ teaspoon ground cinnamon
¼ cup dry red wine
2 cups tomato-based pasta sauce, bottled or homemade
¼ cup chopped fresh flat-leaf parsley
¾ cup soft or silken tofu
2 cups soy milk or milk
½ teaspoon salt
⅛ teaspoon freshly ground black pepper
Pinch of nutmeg
½ cup freshly grated Parmesan or soy Parmesan cheese

Cook the macaroni in a large pot of salted boiling water, stirring occasionally, until it is al dente, about 8 minutes. When the pasta is cooked, drain it and set aside. Heat the oil in a large skillet over medium heat. Add the onion and cook until softened, about 5 minutes. Stir in the garlic, vegetarian burger, oregano, cinnamon, and wine, and simmer to cook off the alcohol. Stir in the pasta sauce and parsley, and cook over low heat for 10 minutes to blend the flavors. While the sauce is cooking, combine the tofu, soy milk, salt, pepper, and nutmeg in a blender or food processor, and blend until well combined.

Preheat the oven to 375°F. Lightly oil a 9-by-13-inch baking dish.

Spread half of the macaroni in the prepared dish and sprinkle with half the cheese. Spread all of the tomato sauce over the top and layer the remaining macaroni over the tomato sauce. Spread the tofu mixture over the top and sprinkle with the remaining cheese. Bake for 40 minutes or until bubbly and lightly browned on top. Let stand at room temperature for 10 minutes before cutting into squares to serve.

*Serves 6 to 8*

OTHER PASTA CHOICES: small shells, orecchiette

# Baked Penne with Broccoli and Tofu

This comforting casserole is a powerhouse of protein, calcium, and vitamin C. For an easy, no-fuss dinner, it can be assembled ahead of time and refrigerated. Simply bring to room temperature before baking.

1 bunch broccoli
12 ounces penne
2 tablespoons olive oil
1 large onion, minced
1 pound firm tofu, crumbled
2 tablespoons tamari soy sauce
1 (28-ounce) can Italian plum tomatoes, finely chopped
½ cup dry red wine
¼ cup chopped fresh flat-leaf parsley
1 teaspoon minced fresh marjoram, or ½ teaspoon dried
½ teaspoon salt
¼ teaspoon freshly ground black pepper
½ cup grated Asiago or soy Parmesan cheese
⅓ cup dried breadcrumbs

Remove the thick stems from the broccoli and discard or reserve for another use. Separate the florets into smaller pieces. Peel the remaining stems with a vegetable peeler and coarsely chop (you should have about 3 cups of florets and chopped broccoli). Set aside. Cook the penne in a large pot of salted boiling water, stirring occasionally, until the pasta is al dente, about 8 to 10 minutes. About 4 or 5 minutes before the pasta is cooked, add the broccoli. When the pasta is cooked, drain the pasta and broccoli and place in a large bowl. Heat 1 tablespoon of the oil in a large skillet over medium-high heat, add the onion, and cook until softened, about 5 minutes. Add the tofu and tamari, and cook until the tofu is lightly browned. Stir in the tomatoes, wine, parsley, marjoram, salt, and pepper, and simmer for 15 to 20 minutes or until the liquid reduces.

Preheat the oven to 375°F. Lightly oil a 2-quart baking dish.

Add the tofu mixture and half of the cheese to the penne and broccoli, and toss to combine. Spoon the mixture into the prepared baking dish. Combine the remaining cheese with the breadcrumbs and the remaining olive oil in a small bowl, and sprinkle over the top of the pasta. Bake for 30 minutes or until hot and lightly browned on top.

*Serves 6*

OTHER PASTA CHOICES: ziti or other tubular pasta

# Pasta-Stuffed Peppers

The ditalini stuffing complements the peppers perfectly and makes a nice change of pace from rice for stuffed pepper enthusiasts. Serve with a green salad and crusty Italian bread for a satisfying meal.

8 ounces ditalini

6 large green or red bell peppers, tops cut off, seeds removed

2 tablespoons olive oil

1 small yellow onion, minced

1 garlic clove, minced

1 (16-ounce) can Italian plum tomatoes, finely chopped

2 tablespoons raisins

2 tablespoons minced fresh flat-leaf parsley

1 teaspoon minced fresh basil, or ½ teaspoon dried

⅛ teaspoon hot red pepper flakes, or to taste

½ teaspoon salt

¼ teaspoon freshly ground black pepper

½ cup dried breadcrumbs

½ cup freshly grated Parmesan or soy Parmesan cheese

Cook the ditalini in a large pot of salted boiling water until it is al dente, about 6 to 8 minutes. When the pasta is cooked, drain it and set aside. Cook the peppers in a large pot of boiling water for 5 minutes to soften them slightly. Drain them and set aside. Heat 1 tablespoon of the olive oil in large skillet over medium heat. Add the onion and cook until soft, about 5 minutes. Add the garlic, tomatoes, raisins, parsley, basil, red pepper flakes, salt, and pepper. Simmer over low heat for 15 minutes to blend the flavors. Combine the cooked ditalini with the tomato sauce in a bowl and mix well. Combine the remaining oil with the breadcrumbs and Parmesan in a small bowl. Toss with a fork and set aside.

Preheat the oven to 375°F. Lightly oil a 2-quart baking dish and add ½ inch of water on the bottom.

Stuff the peppers with the pasta mixture, then sprinkle with the crumb mixture and place in the prepared dish. Cover with foil and bake for 20 minutes or until the peppers are tender. Uncover and bake 5 to 10 minutes longer to brown the topping.

*Serves 6*

OTHER PASTA CHOICES: orzo, stellini

# Lemony Chard-Stuffed Shells

Swiss chard is a member of the beet family and, despite its name, is native to the regions of the Mediterranean. It is especially high in Vitamins A and C, and is rich in iron, calcium, and potassium. If chard is unavailable, spinach may be substituted.

12 large pasta shells

2 tablespoons olive oil

½ cup minced shallots

1 bunch Swiss chard, coarsely chopped (about 3 cups)

4 ounces white mushrooms, chopped (1 cup)

1 pound firm tofu, crumbled

⅓ cup freshly grated Parmesan or soy Parmesan cheese

Juice and zest of 1 lemon

½ teaspoon salt

¼ teaspoon freshly ground black pepper

3 cups tomato-based pasta sauce, bottled or homemade (page 66)

Cook the shells in a large pot of salted boiling water, stirring occasionally, until they are al dente, about 10 minutes. When the pasta is cooked, drain it and set aside. Heat the oil in a large skillet. Add the shallots and cook until softened, about 4 minutes. Add the chard and mushrooms, and cook until just tender, about 3 minutes. Transfer the mixture to a large bowl. Add the tofu, Parmesan, lemon juice and zest, salt, and pepper, and mix well. Preheat the oven to 350°F. Using a teaspoon, stuff the filling into the shells until well packed. Spread a layer of the pasta sauce in the bottom of a shallow 9-by-13-inch baking dish. Arrange the shells on top of the sauce, and pour the remaining sauce over and around the shells. Cover and bake for 30 minutes or until hot.

*Serves 4*

OTHER PASTA CHOICES: manicotti, cannelloni

# Spinach Tortellini with Peas and Hazelnut Gremolata

Adding toasted hazelnuts to the gremolata gives it a rich flavor and textural interest while elevating the dish to company fare. In addition to serving as an entree, this dish would make an elegant first course.

3 large garlic cloves, finely minced
¾ cup chopped fresh flat-leaf parsley
¼ cup chopped hazelnuts, toasted
Zest of 2 lemons
1 pound fresh or frozen spinach tortellini
½ cup frozen peas
¼ cup extra-virgin olive oil
Salt and freshly ground black pepper

Combine the garlic, parsley, hazelnuts, and lemon zest in a small bowl and set aside. Cook the tortellini in a large pot of salted boiling water according to the package directions. During the last minute of cooking time, add the peas. When the pasta is cooked, drain the pasta and peas, and place in a large bowl. Add the oil, the gremolata, and salt and pepper to taste, and toss gently to combine. Transfer to individual serving plates and serve immediately.

*Serves 4*

OTHER PASTA CHOICES: ravioli, raviolini

# Tetrazzini-Style Fettuccine

Based on the early-twentieth-century gratin made with turkey and noodles, this version uses tofu with the requisite sherry and almonds. Although it is named for the famous opera star Luisa Tetrazzini, most authorities agree that it is doubtful that she ever tasted the dish. Steamed green beans, warm dinner rolls, and a fruity white wine round out the meal.

12 ounces fettuccine

2 tablespoons olive oil

3 to 4 shallots, minced

1 pound firm tofu, cut into ½-inch cubes

8 ounces white mushrooms, sliced

¼ cup dry sherry

¼ teaspoon salt

⅛ teaspoon freshly ground black pepper

1 cup vegetable stock

2 tablespoons cornstarch dissolved in 2 tablespoons water

1 cup milk or soy milk

¾ cup slivered toasted almonds

1 cup grated Monterey Jack or soy mozzarella cheese

¼ cup dried breadcrumbs

Cook the fettuccine in a large pot of salted boiling water, stirring occasionally, until it is al dente, about 10 minutes. When the pasta is cooked, drain it and set aside.

Preheat the oven to 375°F. Lightly oil a 9-by-13-inch baking dish.

Heat the oil in large skillet over medium heat. Add the shallots and cook until soft, about 5 minutes. Add the tofu and mushrooms, and cook for 2 to 4 minutes, or until the tofu is lightly browned and the mushrooms are softened. Add the sherry and season with salt and pepper, stirring for 1 minute to cook off the alcohol. Remove from heat and set aside. In a medium saucepan, heat the vegetable stock to a boil, whisk in the cornstarch mixture, stirring to thicken, then reduce heat to low. Slowly stir in the milk or soy milk and set aside. Combine the cooked pasta, the tofu mixture, the almonds, and half of the cheese in a large bowl. Stir in the sauce and mix well. Transfer the mixture to the prepared dish. Sprinkle the top with the remaining cheese and the breadcrumbs. Bake for 30 minutes or until hot.

*Serves 6*

OTHER PASTA CHOICES: linguine, pappardelle

# EARLY ORIGINS OF VEGETARIAN PASTA DISHES

It is interesting to note that many traditional Italian pasta dishes are naturally meatless. There are several reasons for this, including the fact that throughout the ages, much of Italy's population was poor and could not afford meat. When pasta became popular with the more well-to-do strata of society, it was (and still is) eaten as a separate course, often preceding a meat course.

Still another reason for the vast number of traditional meatless pasta recipes is the influence of Catholic fast days, which necessitated many Italian homemakers to find creative ways to prepare pasta with beans and vegetables. In most cases, the resulting dishes were developed according to the ingredients available at the time.

# Pasta Around the World

Fusion food has taken the culinary world by storm—and it's no wonder. The harmonious blending of the world's cuisines creates exciting new ways to enjoy some of our favorite ingredients in nontraditional ways. And pasta is no exception. Infinitely versatile, Italian pastas readily team up with peanut sauce, curry, coconut milk, and other global seasonings with delicious results.

In this chapter, linguine, capellini, and other Italian strands are used to replace Asian noodles in a variety of East meets West fusions. This chapter also includes colorful Middle Eastern pilafs made with orzo, the diminutive rice-shaped pasta (pages 142 and 147), and a satisfying Apricot Noodle Kugel (page 148), as well as the zesty Cumin-Tossed Linguine with Avocado-Tomato Cream (page 137), and Spicy Creole Cavatappi (page 143).

Linguine Vegetable Lo Mein

Fettuccine and Green Beans with Peanut Sauce

Cumin-Tossed Linguine with Avocado-Tomato Cream

Farfalle with Curried Vegetables

Creamy Noodle Curry

Indonesian-Style Capellini

Orzo and Dried Fruit Pilaf with Almonds and Cashews

Spicy Creole Cavatappi

Tangy Tempeh Linguine

Fettuccine Pad Thai

Saffron Orzo Pilaf

Apricot Noodle Kugel

# Linguine Vegetable Lo Mein

Linguine stands in for Chinese lo mein noodles in this popular noodle stir-fry. Vary the vegetables according to personal preference, substituting bok choy for the broccoli or shiitakes for the white mushrooms, if you like.

12 ounces linguine
2 teaspoons dark sesame oil
1 tablespoon vegetable oil
3 scallions, minced
1 garlic clove, minced
2 teaspoons minced fresh ginger
8 ounces extra-firm tofu, cut into ½-inch strips
3 tablespoons tamari soy sauce, or to taste
2 cups broccoli florets
½ cup thinly sliced carrots, cut diagonally
4 ounces white mushrooms, sliced (1 cup)

Cook the linguine in a large pot of salted boiling water until it is al dente, about 8 minutes. When the pasta is cooked, drain it and place in a bowl. Add the sesame oil and toss to coat. Heat the vegetable oil in a large skillet or wok over medium-high heat. Add the scallions, garlic, and ginger, and stir-fry until fragrant, about 30 seconds. Add the tofu and 1 tablespoon of the tamari, and stir-fry until the tofu is lightly browned, about 1 minute. Add the tofu mixture to the linguine and set aside. Reheat the skillet and add the broccoli, carrots, 1 tablespoon of water, and 1 tablespoon of the tamari. Stir-fry until just tender, about 3 minutes. Add the mushrooms and remaining tamari, and stir-fry 1 minute longer. Add the linguine and tofu mixture to the skillet, tossing to combine, and heat through. Add additional tamari if desired and serve immediately.

*Serves 4*

OTHER PASTA CHOICES: fettuccine, spaghetti

# Fettuccine and Green Beans with Peanut Sauce

Peanuts, lime, and chili paste give this dish a taste of Thai. You decide how much or how little chili paste you want to use. Thai beer makes a good accompaniment.

½ cup peanut butter
1 garlic clove, minced
3 tablespoons tamari soy sauce
2 teaspoons brown sugar
1 tablespoon fresh lime juice
½ teaspoon hot chili paste, or to taste
1½ cups vegetable stock or water
12 ounces fettuccine
About 12 ounces green beans, cut into 1-inch pieces (3 cups)
2 tablespoons minced fresh cilantro or Thai basil
2 tablespoons chopped roasted peanuts

In a food processor or blender combine the peanut butter, garlic, tamari, brown sugar, lime juice, chili paste, and ½ cup of the stock or water. Blend until smooth. Transfer the peanut sauce to a saucepan and stir in as much of the remaining stock as needed to give it a smooth, saucelike consistency. Heat the sauce over low heat, stirring until it is hot, then keep it warm over very low heat. Cook the fettuccine in a large pot of salted boiling water, stirring occasionally, until it is al dente, about 10 minutes. When the pasta has cooked for about 3 minutes, add the green beans to the cooking pasta. When the pasta is cooked, drain the pasta and green beans, and place in a serving bowl. Add the peanut sauce and toss to combine. Transfer to individual plates and garnish with cilantro or basil and chopped peanuts and serve immediately.

*Serves 4*

OTHER PASTA CHOICES: **linguine, farfalle**

# Cumin-Tossed Linguine with Avocado-Tomato Cream

Linguine and Southwestern ingredients team up to provide a new interpretation of the Spaghetti Western. For a milder version, cut back on the amount of chiles.

2 tablespoons olive oil
1 small yellow onion, minced
1 or 2 jalapeño or serrano chiles, seeded and chopped
1 garlic clove, minced
2 tablespoons all-purpose flour
1½ cups soy milk or milk
1 cup tomato puree
1 avocado
Juice and zest of 1 lime
1 pound linguine
¾ teaspoon ground cumin, or more to taste
2 tablespoons minced fresh cilantro

Heat the oil in a large skillet over medium heat. Add the onion, chiles, and garlic, and cook until soft, about 5 minutes. Stir in the flour, and gradually add the milk, stirring to thicken. Stir in the tomato puree, reduce heat to low and cook 2 minutes longer . In a food processor or blender, puree the avocado and lime juice with 1 cup of the tomato mixture. Add the remaining tomato mixture to the avocado mixture, and process until smooth. Transfer to a saucepan and keep warm over low heat. Cook the linguine in a large pot of salted boiling water until it is al dente, about 8 minutes. When the pasta is cooked, drain it and place in a large serving bowl. Add the cumin and lime zest, and toss to combine. Top with the sauce, sprinkle with cilantro, and serve immediately.

*Serves 4*

OTHER PASTA CHOICES: fettuccine, spaghetti

# Farfalle with Curried Vegetables

Noodles are not unheard of in India. Among them are *sevian,* which are usually made from chickpea flour and fried and eaten as a snack, and vermicelli prepared as a sweet pudding.

½ cup soft or silken tofu
1½ cups lowfat unsweetened coconut milk
Salt
⅛ teaspoon cayenne pepper
2 tablespoons vegetable oil
1 onion, minced
1 red bell pepper, chopped
2 tablespoons Madras curry powder, or more to taste
½ cup vegetable stock or water
1 pound farfalle
2 cups broccoli florets
1 carrot, sliced
½ cup frozen peas

In a blender combine the tofu with the coconut milk, salt to taste, and cayenne. Blend well and set aside. Heat the oil in a skillet over medium heat. Add the onion and bell pepper, and cook 5 minutes to soften. Stir in the curry powder, and cook until fragrant, about 30 seconds. Add the stock or water and simmer for 5 minutes. Stir in the tofu mixture and keep warm over low heat. Cook the farfalle in a large pot of salted boiling water until it is al dente, about 8 minutes. During the last 5 minutes of cooking time, add the broccoli and carrots to the pasta. About 1 minute before the pasta and vegetables are cooked, add the peas. When the pasta is cooked, drain and transfer to a serving bowl. Add the sauce and toss to combine. Serve immediately.

*Serves 4*

OTHER PASTA CHOICES: penne, ziti

# Creamy Noodle Curry

A mild curry paste may be substituted for the hot, if you prefer. Serve with a choice of condiments on the table: Small bowls containing chutney, chopped peanuts, flaked coconut, scallions, and raisins can be added to suit individual preferences.

1 tablespoon vegetable oil
1 onion, chopped
2 garlic cloves, minced
1½ tablespoons hot curry paste, or to taste
1 (15-ounce) can diced tomatoes
1½ cups cooked chickpeas, drained and rinsed
½ cup soft or silken tofu
½ cups lowfat unsweetened coconut milk
Salt and freshly ground black pepper
1 pound fettuccine
8 ounces green beans, cut into 1-inch pieces (2 cups)

Heat the oil in a large skillet over medium heat. Add the onion and cook for 5 minutes to soften. Stir in the garlic and curry paste, and cook 2 minutes, stirring to blend. Stir in the tomatoes and their liquid, and simmer for 5 minutes to blend flavors. Add the chickpeas and keep warm over low heat. In a food processor or blender, combine the tofu with the coconut milk, and add salt and pepper to taste. Blend until smooth. Stir the tofu mixture into the vegetable mixture and keep warm over low heat. Cook the fettuccine in a large pot of salted boiling water, stirring occasionally, until it is al dente, about 10 minutes. When the pasta has cooked for about 3 minutes, add the green beans. When the pasta is cooked, drain the fettuccine and green beans, and place in a large serving bowl. Add the curried vegetables and toss to combine. Serve immediately.

*Serves 4*

OTHER PASTA CHOICES: linguine, spaghetti

# Indonesian-Style Capellini

Tempeh is made from compressed soybeans that are formed into cakes. It originated in Indonesia, so it is especially suited to complement the Indonesian seasonings. Thin strands of capellini are used here instead of the traditional rice vermicelli, to good effect. Adjust the cayenne according to taste or omit it and use hot chile paste or fresh chiles instead.

8 ounces tempeh, cut into ½-inch dice
2 tablespoons vegetable oil
2 tablespoons tamari soy sauce
⅓ cup creamy peanut butter
⅓ cup lowfat unsweetened coconut milk
⅓ cup vegetable stock or water
1 tablespoon lime juice
¼ teaspoon cayenne pepper, or to taste
1 bunch scallions, chopped
½ bell pepper, chopped
1 tablespoon minced fresh ginger
1 cup frozen peas, thawed
12 ounces capellini
1 tablespoon dark sesame oil
¼ cup chopped peanuts
2 tablespoons minced cilantro

Poach the tempeh in a small saucepan of simmering water for 5 to 7 minutes. Drain it and blot dry. Heat 1 tablespoon of the oil in a large skillet over medium-high heat. Add the tempeh and cook until browned on all sides, about 5 minutes, adding 1 tablespoon of the tamari to add color and flavor. Remove the tempeh from the skillet and set aside. In a food processor, combine the peanut butter, coconut milk, stock or water, lime juice, cayenne, and the remaining tablespoon of tamari. Process until smooth, then set aside. Heat the remaining tablespoon of oil in the skillet over medium heat. Add the scallions, bell pepper, and ginger, and cook, stirring occasionally, until the pepper is softened, about 5 minutes. Reduce heat to low, stir in the peas, and add the tempeh. Stir in the peanut sauce and simmer over low heat while the pasta is cooking. Cook the capellini in a large pot of salted boiling water, stirring occasionally, until it is al dente, about 2 to 4 minutes. When the pasta is cooked, drain it and place in a large bowl. Add the sesame oil and the tempeh and vegetable mixture, and toss gently to combine. Divide the pasta among individual plates and serve immediately, garnished with chopped peanuts and minced cilantro.

*Serves 4*

OTHER PASTA CHOICES: vermicelli, spaghettini, angel hair

# Orzo and Dried Fruit Pilaf with Almonds and Cashews

Orzo, the diminutive rice-shaped pasta, makes an interesting change from rice. The sweetness of dates and raisins plays nicely off the toasty crunch of almonds and cashews in this flavorful Middle Eastern-style pilaf.

2 cups orzo
1 tablespoon olive oil
1 small yellow onion, minced
2 scallions, minced
1 carrot, shredded
½ cup frozen peas, thawed
½ cup chopped pitted dates
¼ cup golden raisins
⅛ teaspoon ground allspice
Salt and freshly ground black pepper
¼ cup minced fresh flat-leaf parsley
½ cup slivered almonds, toasted
¼ cup chopped cashews, toasted

Cook the orzo in a large pot of salted boiling water, stirring occasionally, until it is al dente, about 6 to 8 minutes. When the orzo is cooked, drain and set aside. Heat the oil in a large skillet over medium heat. Add the onion and cook until softened, about 5 minutes. Add the scallions, carrot, and peas, and cook until the vegetables are soft, about 5 minutes. Stir in the orzo, dates, raisins, allspice, and salt and pepper to taste, stirring to combine and heat through, about 5 minutes. Stir in the parsley, almonds, and cashews, and serve immediately.

*Serves 4*

OTHER PASTA CHOICES: stellini, ditalini

# Spicy Creole Cavatappi

Pasta served with hot spicy sauce like this one makes a piquant change.

2 tablespoons olive oil
1 large onion, chopped
1 stalk celery, chopped
1 large green bell pepper, chopped
2 garlic cloves, minced
2 tablespoons tomato paste
1 (28-ounce) can Italian plum tomatoes, chopped
½ cup water
1 bay leaf
1 teaspoon dried thyme, crumbled
1 teaspoon Tabasco sauce
1 teaspoon filé powder
⅛ teaspoon cayenne pepper
Salt and freshly ground black pepper
8 ounces cooked vegetarian burger crumbles
1 pound cavatappi

Heat the oil in large saucepan over medium heat. Add the onion, celery, and bell pepper. Cover and cook until soft, about 7 minutes. Remove lid, stir in the garlic and tomato paste, and cook 1 minute. Add the tomatoes, water, bay leaf, thyme, Tabasco, filé powder, cayenne, and salt and pepper to taste. Bring to a boil, then reduce heat to low, add the vegetarian burger, and simmer for 15 minutes. Discard the bay leaf and keep the sauce warm over low heat. Cook the cavatappi in a large pot of salted boiling water, stirring occasionally, until it is al dente, about 8 to 10 minutes. When the pasta is cooked, drain it and transfer to individual plates or shallow bowls. Top with the sauce and serve immediately.

*Serves 4*

OTHER PASTA CHOICES: fusilli, gemelli

# Tangy Tempeh Linguine

Noodle stir-fries are common to virtually all Asian cuisines–lo mein of China, Thailand's pad thai, and Indonesian *bahmie goreng,* to name a few. This Asian fusion dish uses linguine noodles but features elements from several Asian countries including meaty chunks of Indonesian tempeh, Chinese hoisin sauce, and Japanese sake.

1 (8-ounce) package tempeh, cut into ½-inch cubes

6 tablespoons hoisin sauce

2 tablespoons tamari soy sauce

2 tablespoons water

1 tablespoon sake or dry white wine

12 ounces linguine

1 teaspoon dark sesame oil

2 tablespoons vegetable oil

3 cups (about 1 pound) coarsely chopped bok choy

¼ cup minced shallots

1 tablespoon minced fresh ginger

¼ teaspoon hot red pepper flakes

Poach the tempeh in a small saucepan of simmering water for 5 to 7 minutes. Drain it, blot dry, and set aside. Combine the hoisin, tamari, water, and sake in a small bowl until well blended. Set aside. Cook the linguine in a large pot of salted boiling water, stirring occasionally, until it is al dente, about 8 minutes. When the pasta is cooked, drain it and place in a bowl. Add the sesame oil, toss to combine, and set aside. Heat 1 tablespoon of the vegetable oil in a skillet or wok over medium-high heat. Add the tempeh and stir-fry quickly to brown it on all sides. Remove immediately with a slotted spoon. Reheat the wok or skillet over medium heat with the remaining 1 tablespoon oil. Add the bok choy, shallots, ginger, and red pepper flakes, and stir for about 20 seconds, or until the bok choy is wilted. Stir in the hoisin mixture, tempeh, and linguine, and cook, stirring, until heated through, about 1 minute. Transfer to a large shallow serving bowl or individual plates and serve immediately.

*Serves 4*

OTHER PASTA CHOICES: spaghetti, fettuccine

# Fettuccine Pad Thai

This popular Thai noodle dish is made here with fettuccine. It can be spiced up with the addition of hot sauce, chili paste, or hot red pepper flakes.

12 ounces fettuccine
2 tablespoons vegetable oil
8 ounces extra-firm tofu, cut into ½-inch strips
2 tablespoons tamari soy sauce
1 small bell pepper, cut into thin strips
1 bunch scallions, minced
1 garlic clove, minced
1 tomato, cut into eighths
2 tablespoons light brown sugar
2 tablespoons white vinegar
½ cup fresh bean sprouts
¼ cup chopped peanuts

Cook the fettuccine in a large pot of salted boiling water, stirring occasionally, until it is al dente, about 10 minutes. When the pasta is cooked, drain it and place in a bowl. Toss with a small amount of oil and set aside. Heat 1 tablespoon of the oil in a large skillet or wok over medium-high heat. Add the tofu and stir-fry until lightly browned, about 5 minutes. Splash the tofu with 1 tablespoon of the tamari, stirring to coat. Remove from the skillet and set aside. Reheat the skillet or wok over medium heat with the remaining 1 tablespoon of oil. Add the bell pepper, scallions, and garlic, and stir-fry until softened, about 5 minutes. Add the tomato, sugar, vinegar, and the remaining tamari. Cook about 3 minutes to blend the flavors. Add the fettuccine and tofu, and toss gently to combine and heat through. Divide among individual plates, sprinkle with bean sprouts and peanuts, and serve immediately.

*Serves 4*

OTHER PASTA CHOICES: **linguine, spaghetti**

# Saffron Orzo Pilaf

Saffron strands are the dried stigmas of the crocus flower. Although it gives a lovely yellow hue to the orzo, saffron can be exorbitantly expensive. Powdered saffron is somewhat less pricey than the strands, but turmeric is cheaper still and may be substituted for a fraction of the cost. Use turmeric judiciously, however, as its dusky flavor can sometimes interfere with the flavors in a recipe. If you use the saffron strands, dissolve them in a bowl with two tablespoons of hot water.

2 cups orzo
1 tablespoon olive oil
½ red bell pepper, chopped
1 zucchini, chopped
1 carrot, shredded
1 bunch scallions, minced
⅛ teaspoon saffron powder or turmeric
¼ cup chopped fresh flat-leaf parsley
Salt and freshly ground black pepper

Cook the orzo in a large pot of salted boiling water, stirring occasionally, until it is al dente, about 6 to 8 minutes. When the orzo is cooked, drain it and set aside. Heat the oil in a large skillet over medium heat. Add the bell pepper, zucchini, carrot, and scallions, and cook until softened, about 5 minutes. Add the orzo and saffron or turmeric, and stir to combine. Stir in the parsley and season with salt and pepper to taste. Serve immediately in a large shallow serving bowl.

*Serves 4*

OTHER PASTA CHOICES: ditalini, stellini

# Apricot Noodle Kugel

Despite its slight sweetness, noodle pudding, or kugel, is traditionally eaten as a side dish. They are eaten throughout Eastern Europe and in Israel as well as in the United States, where they are often included on menus during Hanukkah.

1 cup dried apricots
8 ounces fettuccine
1 cup golden raisins
½ cup chopped dates
1 tablespoon vegetable oil
1 cup soft or silken tofu
2 cups soy milk or milk
1 teaspoon cinnamon
½ teaspoon allspice
½ cup sugar, or a natural sweetener
Pinch of salt
½ cup coarsely ground almonds

Place the apricots in a heatproof bowl and cover with boiling water. Let stand for 30 minutes to plump, then drain and chop them. Set aside. Cook the fettuccine in a large pot of salted boiling water, stirring occasionally, until it is soft, about 12 minutes. When the pasta is cooked, drain it and place in a large bowl along with the raisins, dates, and apricots. Add the oil and toss to coat.

Preheat the oven to 350°F. Lightly oil a 9-by-13-inch baking dish.

In a blender combine the tofu, soy milk, cinnamon, allspice, sugar, and salt, and blend until smooth. Stir the tofu mixture into the noodle mixture until well combined, then transfer the mixture to the prepared dish. Top with the ground almonds and bake for 45 minutes, or until lightly browned. Let the kugel stand for at least 1 hour before cutting into squares.

*Serves 4*

OTHER PASTA CHOICES: pappardelle, lasagna

# PASTA TO THE RESCUE

Keep a few jars of commercial pasta sauces on hand for dinner emergencies. They can provide a good starting point for quick and easy meals. Often, just a splash of red wine, some sliced mushrooms, olives, or fresh herbs can give these products a fresh, homemade taste. Since some brands of sauce are better than others, it's a good idea to experiment until you find one that is reliable and full of flavor.

# Soup Makes the Meal

The addition of pasta can turn a simple bowl of vegetable soup into a hearty one-dish meal. Soups can surround a variety of pasta shapes from the diminutive made-for-soup pastinas such as ditalini, orzo, and stellini, to elbow macaroni, on up to thick fettuccine noodles.

Recipes for stick-to-your-ribs bean soups, such as Pasta Fagiole (page 153), Lentil Soup with Chard and Orzo (page 159), and Tuscan White Bean Soup with Ditalini (page 158) will be warming winter favorites, along with two versions of the classic minestrone. For something different, try Noodle Soup in Shiitake-Ginger Broth (page 163) or put on a pot of Tastes Like Chicken Noodle Soup (page 164) for a taste of childhood nostalgia.

Since the flavor of most soup improves with time, plan to make these soups the day before serving for a quick supper the following day.

Note: In recipes calling for vegetable stock, you can use homemade stock, commercially prepared broth, or a vegetable broth powder or cube, prepared according to the package directions. Since seasonings vary greatly among brands, monitor your use of salt carefully, adjusting as necessary.

Pasta Fagiole

Minestrone with Pesto

Starstruck Minestrone with Yellow Peppers and Chickpeas

Tuscan White Bean Soup with Ditalini

Lentil Soup with Chard and Orzo

Tortellini Escarole Soup

Tomato-Basil Soup with "Peppercorn" Pasta

Vegetable Noodle Soup

Noodle Soup in Shiitake-Ginger Broth

Tastes Like Chicken Noodle Soup

Ravioli in Leek and Mushroom Essence

Garlic Soup with Pasta Squares

# Pasta Fagiole

Nearly every Friday when I was a child, I'd come home from school to find a pot of "pasta fazool" simmering on the stove. To this day, whenever I make this popular pasta and bean soup, a flood of memories comes rushing back.

2 tablespoons olive oil

1 onion, minced

1 large garlic clove, minced

1 (6-ounce) can tomato paste

Salt and freshly ground black pepper

¼ teaspoon dried oregano

1 bay leaf

6 cups vegetable stock or water

3 cups cooked light red or white kidney beans, drained and rinsed

8 ounces elbow macaroni

Freshly grated Parmesan or soy Parmesan cheese

Heat the oil in a large pot over medium heat. Add the onion and cook for 5 to 7 minutes or until soft. Add the garlic and cook 1 minute. Reduce heat to low and blend in the tomato paste. Add the oregano, bay leaf, stock, and salt and pepper to taste, and simmer over low heat for about 30 minutes. Stir in the beans. Meanwhile, cook the macaroni in a large pot of salted boiling water, stirring occasionally, until it is just al dente, about 6 to 8 minutes. When the pasta is cooked, drain it and stir it into the bean mixture. Simmer gently for 10 minutes to blend the flavors. Ladle the soup into bowls, passing a bowl of grated cheese at the table.

*Serves 6 to 8*

OTHER PASTA CHOICES: small shells, radiatore

# Minestrone with Pesto

In both Milan and Genoa, a swirl of pesto is added near the end of cooking time to enrich this classic soup. If you prefer, instead of adding the cooked pastina to the soup pot, you can place a large spoonful into the bottom of the soup bowls at serving time, and ladle the hot soup over the tiny pasta.

    2 tablespoons olive oil
    3 garlic cloves, minced
    1 large onion, minced
    2 carrots, cut into ¼-inch slices
    ½ small cabbage, shredded
    1 potato, diced
    1 (14-ounce) can tomatoes, chopped
    2 tablespoons tomato paste
    7 cups vegetable stock or water
    1 teaspoon dried basil
    ½ teaspoon dried oregano
    Salt and freshly ground black pepper
    1½ cups cooked cannellini beans, drained and rinsed
    1 zucchini, sliced thin
    4 ounces fresh green beans, trimmed and cut in half (about 1 cup)
    1 cup anellini (little rings)
    2 tablespoons chopped fresh flat-leaf parsley
    ½ cup pesto (page 110)

Heat the oil in a large stockpot over medium heat, and add the garlic, onion, carrots, and cabbage. Cook, stirring, for about 10 minutes. Add the potato, tomatoes, tomato paste, stock or water, basil, oregano, and salt and pepper to taste. Bring the mixture to a boil, reduce heat, and simmer for 30 minutes. Stir in the cannellini beans, zucchini, and green beans, and cook for another 20 minutes. Cook the anellini in a large pot of salted boiling water, stirring occasionally, until it is al dente, about 5 minutes. When the pasta is cooked, drain it and stir into the soup along with the parsley. Simmer gently for 10 minutes to blend the flavors. To serve, ladle the soup into bowls and top with a swirl of pesto.

*Serves 6 to 8*

OTHER PASTA CHOICES:  ditalini, stellini

# Starstruck Minestrone with Yellow Peppers and Chickpeas

Some version of minestrone or other hearty soup is eaten on a daily basis throughout Southern Italy, usually as the evening meal. Calabria, located at the "toe of the boot" is no exception. The inclusion of yellow bell peppers is typically Calabrese.

2 tablespoons olive oil

1 large onion, minced

1 carrot, chopped

1 large yellow bell pepper, chopped

1 stalk celery, including leaves, chopped

3 cloves garlic, minced

1 (16-ounce) can tomatoes, chopped

7 cups vegetable stock or water

1 bay leaf

1 teaspoon fresh savory, or ¼ teaspoon dried

1 teaspoon fresh marjoram, or ¼ teaspoon dried

Salt and freshly ground black pepper

1 pound fresh spinach, coarsely chopped (about 2 cups)

1½ cups cooked chickpeas, drained and rinsed

2 tablespoons chopped fresh flat-leaf parsley

1 cup stellini

Freshly grated Parmesan or soy Parmesan cheese

Heat the oil in a large stockpot over medium heat. Add the onion, carrot, bell pepper, celery, and garlic, and cook until soft, about 10 minutes. Add the tomatoes, stock or water, bay leaf, savory, marjoram, and salt and pepper to taste. Bring to a boil, reduce heat, and simmer for 30 minutes. Add the spinach, chickpeas, and parsley, and cook another 15 minutes. Meanwhile, cook the stellini in a large pot of salted boiling water, stirring occasionally, until it is al dente, about 5 minutes. When the pasta is cooked, drain it and stir it into the soup. Simmer gently for 5 to 10 minutes to blend the flavors. Ladle the soup into bowls and top with freshly grated Parmesan, if you like.

*Serves 6 to 8*

OTHER PASTA CHOICES: acini de pepe, ditalini

# Tuscan White Bean Soup with Ditalini

The people of Tuscany are known as "bean eaters" owing to the popularity of legumes in their cooking. In addition to the creamy cannellini bean, Tuscans favor chickpeas, favas, and borlotti beans, which are also known as cranberry or Roman beans.

1 tablespoon olive oil
1 onion, minced
1 stalk celery, minced
1 large garlic clove, minced
¼ cup tomato paste
1 (15-ounce) can diced tomatoes
1½ cups cooked cannellini beans, drained and rinsed
½ teaspoon salt, or to taste
Cayenne pepper
¼ teaspoon dried oregano
7 cups vegetable stock or water
8 ounces ditalini
Freshly grated Parmesan or soy Parmesan cheese

Heat the oil in a stockpot over medium heat. Add the onion and celery, and cook until soft, about 5 minutes. Add the garlic and cook for 30 seconds. Blend in the tomato paste. Add the diced tomatoes, beans, salt, cayenne to taste, oregano, and stock or water. Simmer over low heat for 30 minutes. Meanwhile, cook the ditalini in a large pot of salted boiling water, stirring occasionally, until it is al dente, about 5 minutes. When the pasta is cooked, drain it and stir it into the soup. Simmer gently for 10 minutes to blend the flavors. Ladle the soup into bowls, sprinkle with cheese, and serve immediately.

*Serves 6 to 8*

OTHER PASTA CHOICES: **elbows, small shells**

# Lentil Soup with Chard and Orzo

Although chard is often called "Swiss" chard after a Swiss botanist, it is actually a Mediterranean vegetable. Nutrient-rich chard and lentils combine for a healthful wintertime soup with a rich complex flavor.

2 tablespoons olive oil
1 onion, minced
1 carrot, grated
½ cup minced celery
2 garlic cloves, minced
7 cups vegetable stock or water
1 cup dried brown lentils
2 tablespoons tomato paste
½ cup dry red wine
½ cup minced fresh flat-leaf parsley
½ teaspoon minced fresh thyme, or ¼ teaspoon dried
Salt and freshly ground black pepper
4 to 6 ounces Swiss chard, coarsely chopped (about 2 cups)
¾ cup orzo

Heat the oil in a stockpot over medium heat. Add the onion, carrot, celery, and garlic. Cover and cook for 5 minutes. Add the stock or water, lentils, tomato paste, wine, parsley, thyme, and salt and pepper to taste. Bring to a boil, then reduce heat and simmer until the lentils are tender, stirring occasionally, about 30 minutes. About 10 minutes before the soup is cooked, stir in the chard. Meanwhile, cook the orzo in a large pot of salted boiling water, stirring occasionally, until it is al dente, about 5 minutes. When the orzo is cooked, drain it and set aside. When ready to serve, stir the orzo into the hot soup, then ladle it into bowls.

*Serves 6 to 8*

OTHER PASTA CHOICES: stellini, ditalini

# Tortellini Escarole Soup

The name origin of many Italian foods is associated with colorful stories and tortellini is no exception. According to legend, tortellini was created by a Bolognese innkeeper who was so inspired by Venus that he shaped the pasta to resemble her navel. This soup may also be made with chicory or spinach in place of the escarole, if you prefer.

1 tablespoon olive oil
1 onion, chopped
2 carrots, chopped
1 large garlic clove, pressed
1 head escarole, coarsely chopped
6 cups vegetable stock or water
1½ cups cooked cannellini beans, drained and rinsed
½ teaspoon dried marjoram
Salt and freshly ground black pepper
1 cup small, dried cheese tortellini

Heat the oil in a large stockpot over medium heat. Add the onion, carrot, and garlic, and cook covered for 5 minutes to soften the vegetables. Add the escarole and stock or water, and simmer for 15 minutes. Stir in the beans, marjoram, and salt and pepper to taste. Simmer for 15 minutes. Meanwhile, cook the tortellini in a large pot of salted boiling water according to package directions until just tender. When the pasta is cooked, drain it and add to the hot soup just before serving.

*Serves 4 to 6*

OTHER PASTA CHOICES: farfalle, cavatelli

# Tomato-Basil Soup with "Peppercorn" Pasta

Tiny acini de pepe are so named because they resemble peppercorns. For a smoother, more elegant texture, pass the soup through a food mill or fine mesh strainer before combining with the pasta.

1 tablespoon olive oil
1 onion, chopped
¼ cup minced celery
2 garlic cloves, pressed
2 tablespoons tomato paste
3 cups vegetable stock or water
2 (28-ounce) cans crushed plum tomatoes
¼ teaspoon hot red pepper flakes
1 bay leaf
Salt and freshly ground black pepper
1 cup *acini de pepe* (peppercorn pasta)
⅓ cup minced fresh basil

Heat the oil in a large stockpot over medium heat. Add the onion and celery. Cover and cook until softened, about 5 minutes. Add the garlic and cook 1 minute longer. Stir in the tomato paste. Add the stock or water, tomatoes, red pepper flakes, and bay leaf, and bring to boil. Season with salt and pepper to taste. Reduce heat to low and simmer for 30 minutes, stirring occasionally. Cook the pasta in a large pot of salted boiling water until it is tender, about 5 minutes. When the pasta is cooked, drain it and add it to the soup just prior to serving, along with the fresh basil.

*Serves 4 to 6*

OTHER PASTA CHOICES: ditalini, stellini

# Vegetable Noodle Soup

This comforting soup can be altered easily to suit your taste. For example, vary the vegetables according to personal preference, add a can of chickpeas or other beans for extra substance and protein, or spice it up with a pinch of hot red pepper flakes.

8 ounces fettuccine
2 tablespoons olive oil
1 onion, chopped
2 carrots, cut into ¼-inch dice
7 cups vegetable stock or water
4 ounces fresh green beans, cut into 1-inch pieces (1 cup)
3 cups coarsely chopped green cabbage
1 (15-ounce) can diced tomatoes
1 tablespoon minced fresh flat-leaf parsley
Salt and freshly ground black pepper
½ cup frozen peas

Break the fettuccine into 3- to 4-inch pieces and cook in a large pot of salted boiling water, stirring occasionally, until it is al dente, about 10 minutes. When the pasta is cooked, drain it and place in a bowl. Add 1 tablespoon of the oil, toss to combine, and set aside. In a large stockpot, heat the remaining tablespoon of oil over medium-high heat. Add the onion and carrots. Cover and cook until the vegetables soften, about 5 to 7 minutes. Remove cover and add the stock or water, the green beans, cabbage, tomatoes, parsley, and salt and pepper to taste. Simmer for 20 minutes or until the vegetables are tender and the liquid reduces slightly. Stir in the peas and fettuccine. Simmer for 5 minutes to blend the flavors before ladling the soup into bowls.

*Serves 6*

OTHER PASTA CHOICES: linguine, spaghetti

# Noodle Soup in Shiitake-Ginger Broth

Linguine noodles and shiitake mushrooms swim in a broth flavored with ginger and a hint of sesame oil in this Asian-flavored soup. Once the miso paste has been added to the broth, be sure it does not return to a boil, as boiling will destroy the beneficial enzymes in the miso.

8 ounces linguine
1 teaspoon dark sesame oil
6 cups vegetable stock or water
4 ounces shiitake mushrooms, thinly sliced
1 tablespoon minced fresh ginger
1 bunch scallions, finely minced
2 tablespoons tamari or other soy sauce
1 tablespoon white miso paste
1 tablespoon minced fresh parsley

Cook the linguine in a large pot of boiling salted water until it is al dente, about 8 minutes. When the pasta is cooked, drain it and place in a bowl. Add the sesame oil, toss to coat the pasta, and set aside. Bring the vegetable stock or water to a boil in a large saucepan with the shiitakes, ginger, scallions, and tamari. Reduce heat to low and simmer 5 minutes or until the shiitakes soften. Blend the miso paste with ¼ cup of the hot broth in a small bowl. Stir the miso mixture into the soup, add the linguine, sprinkle with parsley, and serve.

*Serves 4*

OTHER PASTA CHOICES: fettuccine, vermicelli

# *Tastes Like Chicken Noodle Soup*

My friend B. J. Atkinson created this recipe, which is one of her family's favorites. It has all the flavor of the rich chicken noodle soup you remember . . . without the bird, of course. B. J. uses Frontier brand vegetarian chicken-flavored broth powder to make this recipe, which is widely available in natural foods stores, both in bulk and individually packaged. If you use another brand, you may need to adjust the amount used. Taste carefully as you cook and don't oversalt.

8 ounces linguine
1 tablespoon olive oil
8 cups water
3 carrots, sliced
½ large onion, chopped
2 stalks celery, halved lengthwise and sliced diagonally,
   plus leaves from one inner stalk, minced
2 large garlic cloves, pressed
¼ cup minced fresh flat-leaf parsley
2 bay leaves
1 tablespoon cornstarch
½ cup vegetarian chicken-flavored broth powder (see note above)
½ cup cool water
¼ teaspoon turmeric
Salt and freshly ground black pepper

Break the linguine strands into thirds and cook in a large pot of salted boiling water until tender, about 8 minutes, stirring frequently to prevent the pasta from sticking together. When the pasta is cooked, drain it and place in a bowl. Add the oil, toss to combine, and set aside. Bring the 8 cups water to a boil in a large stockpot. Add the carrots, onion, celery, garlic, parsley, and bay leaves. Reduce heat to medium and simmer gently for 20 minutes, or until the carrots are tender. In a small bowl, whisk together the cornstarch, vegetarian chicken-flavored broth powder, and ½ cup water, whisking until smooth. When the carrots and other vegetables are tender, stir in the broth mixture and the turmeric. Add the cooked linguine and season with salt and pepper to taste. Simmer the soup for 5 minutes before serving.

*Serves 6 to 8*

OTHER PASTA CHOICES: fettuccine, spaghetti

# Ravioli in Leek and Mushroom Essence

The porcini mushrooms and dry vermouth add depth to the delicate broth in this soup. Look for frozen tofu ravioli in natural foods stores. I like to serve this as a light but elegant entree, preceded by a substantial appetizer such as black olive bruschetta, accompanied by a dry white wine, and finished with a rich dessert.

2 tablespoons olive oil
1 leek, white part only, minced
4 ounces porcini mushrooms, sliced thin
6 cups vegetable stock
2 tablespoons dry vermouth
Salt and freshly ground black pepper
1 pound frozen tofu or cheese ravioli
1 tablespoon snipped fresh chives

Heat 1 tablespoon of the oil in a large stockpot over medium heat. Add the leek and cook until softened, about 4 minutes. Add the mushrooms and cook until slightly softened, about 2 minutes longer. Add the vegetable stock and vermouth, and bring to a boil. Reduce heat to low and simmer until the liquid reduces by about 1 cup, about 20 minutes. Strain the broth through a fine mesh strainer into a saucepan, reserving the solids. In a small skillet heat the remaining 1 tablespoon of oil over medium heat. Add the leek and mushroom solids, cook for 1 minute, season with salt and pepper to taste, and keep warm over low heat. Cook the ravioli in a large pot of salted boiling water according to the package directions. When the pasta is cooked, drain it, divide among individual shallow bowls, and surround with the hot broth. Top with a spoonful of the mushroom and leek mixture and sprinkle with chives. Serve immediately.

*Serves 4*

OTHER PASTA CHOICES : cheese tortellini, gnocchi

# Garlic Soup with Pasta Squares

Both garlic and soup have long been used as home remedies for colds, so combining them would seem to be a surefire cure! Long, slow simmering helps to mellow out the flavor of the garlic. Tiny pasta squares called quadretti add substance to this restorative soup.

10 to 12 garlic cloves
2 tablespoons extra-virgin olive oil
5 cups vegetable stock
Salt
Cayenne pepper
1 cup quadretti
2 tablespoons dry sherry

In a blender or food processor, puree the garlic and olive oil until smooth. Transfer to a large saucepan and cook over medium heat until very fragrant, about 3 minutes, being careful not to brown the garlic. Stir in the stock and salt and cayenne to taste, and bring to boil. Reduce heat and simmer for about 20 to 30 minutes. Meanwhile, cook the quadretti in a large pot of salted boiling water until it is al dente, about 5 minutes. When the pasta is cooked, drain it and divide among soup bowls. Add the sherry to the soup, ladle it into the bowls, and serve immediately.

*Serves 4*

OTHER PASTA CHOICES: **ditalini, stellini**

# A PASTA HERETIC

During the fifteenth century, not everyone was captivated by the pleasures of pasta. There was a Florentine monk and religious fanatic named Girolamo Savonarola who spoke with fiery condemnation concerning pasta eating. He thought plain boiled pasta was all that was necessary for sustenance and that further embellishment with sauce or seasoning was wickedly indulgent. The people of Florence eventually tired of his rantings, and he was burned at the stake.

# Cool Salads for Warm Days

A far cry from the mayonnaise-laden macaroni salad of a bygone era, today's pasta salads are light, fresh, and full of flavor. Paired with a variety of vegetables, fruits, and other ingredients and tossed in delicate vinaigrettes, these lighter pasta salads are summertime favorites. Versatile, colorful, and bursting with flavor, pasta salads also make ideal party fare and look great on a buffet table. Easy to transport, pasta salads are popular choices for picnics and potlucks.

Among the varied recipes in this chapter are Lime-Dressed Vermicelli with Green Papaya and Peanuts (page 173), and Artichoke Pasta Salad with Balsamic Vinaigrette (page 178).

Portion size for pasta salads can be tricky, depending on the situation. Some are chock full of vegetables and beans and would make good entrees, while others that are less substantial are more appropriate as side dishes. When making a pasta salad for a buffet, consider what other foods will be served to help you decide on quantity. The portion sizes listed in the recipes are for entree servings.

Remember, one of the few times it's okay to rinse pasta is when it's being used in a salad.

Lime-Dressed Vermicelli with Green Papaya and Peanuts

Cold Noodle Salad with Peanut Sauce

Chilled Pasta Niçoise

Three-Pepper Pasta Salad

Ratatouille Radiatore

Artichoke Pasta Salad with Balsamic Vinaigrette

Lighten Up Macaroni Salad

Summer Sunshine Pasta Salad

Fruity Tropical Pasta Salad

Cumin-Spiced Pasta Salad with Jalapeño Pesto

Pinto Bean and Salsa Pasta Toss with Lime and Avocado

Spicy Cucumber Pasta Salad

# Lime-Dressed Vermicelli with Green Papaya and Peanuts

Long thin shreds of papaya and carrot look best in this refreshing salad. Make them yourself with a mandoline slicer or look for them in the produce section of well-stocked Asian markets. Those with milder tastes may cut down on or eliminate the red pepper flakes. However, hot food lovers might prefer substituting fresh minced Thai birdseye chiles for a jolt of extra-fiery heat.

12 ounces vermicelli
½ cup dark sesame oil
Juice and zest of 1 lime
2 garlic cloves, minced
2 tablespoons rice wine vinegar
2 teaspoons grated fresh ginger
¼ teaspoon hot red pepper flakes, or to taste
Salt
1 green papaya, shredded
1 carrot, shredded
4 scallions, minced
½ cup chopped peanuts

Cook the vermicelli in a large pot of salted boiling water, stirring occasionally, until it is al dente, about 2 to 4 minutes. When the pasta is cooked, drain it, rinse with cold water, and place in a large serving bowl. Add 1 tablespoon of the sesame oil, toss to combine, and set aside. To make the dressing, combine the remaining oil, the lime juice and zest, garlic, vinegar, ginger, red pepper flakes, and salt in a small bowl. Add the papaya, carrot, scallions, and dressing to the pasta and toss together. Sprinkle with chopped peanuts before serving.

*Serves 4*

OTHER PASTA CHOICES: capellini, spaghetti, angel hair

# Cold Noodle Salad with Peanut Sauce

The creamy peanut sauce makes this salad popular at parties, where it goes well with vegetable spring rolls and tempeh satays. Add to or decrease the chili paste according to personal taste.

12 ounces linguine
2 tablespoons dark sesame oil
½ cup peanut butter
1 garlic clove, pressed
⅓ cup tamari soy sauce
¼ cup water
1 teaspoon hot chili paste, or to taste
1 (8-ounce) can sliced water chestnuts
1 red bell pepper, cut into thin strips
1 cucumber, peeled, halved lengthwise, seeded, and thinly sliced
¼ cup minced scallions

Cook the linguine in large pot of salted boiling water, stirring occasionally, until it is al dente, about 8 to 10 minutes. When the pasta is cooked, drain it, rinse with cold water, and place in a large serving bowl. Add 1 tablespoon of the sesame oil, toss to combine, cover, and refrigerate. Combine the peanut butter, garlic, remaining 1 table-spoon sesame oil, tamari, water, and chili paste in a small bowl. Add the water chest-nuts, bell pepper, cucumber, scallions, and peanut sauce to the linguine. Toss gently to combine, and serve.

*Serves 4*

OTHER PASTA CHOICES: vermicelli, spaghetti

# Chilled Pasta Niçoise

Classic *salade Niçoise* ingredients team up with penne pasta for a great-tasting Mediterranean fusion salad perfect for al fresco dining. Grill some portobello mushrooms and crusty bread, and dinner is served.

1 pound penne
½ cup extra-virgin olive oil
8 ounces fresh green beans (2 cups), blanched
1½ cups cooked cannellini beans, drained and rinsed
1 cup halved cherry tomatoes
½ cup Niçoise olives, pitted
¼ cup minced fresh flat-leaf parsley
¼ cup white wine vinegar
1 garlic clove, pressed
2 teaspoons Dijon mustard
½ teaspoon salt
Freshly ground black pepper
Salad greens, for serving

Cook the penne in a large pot of salted boiling water, stirring occasionally, until it is al dente, about 8 to 10 minutes. When the pasta is cooked, drain it, rinse under cold water, and place in a large bowl. Toss with 1 tablespoon of the oil and add the green beans, cannellini beans, tomatoes, olives, and parsley. To make the dressing, combine the vinegar, garlic, mustard, salt, and pepper to taste in a small bowl. Whisk in the remaining oil and add to the pasta and vegetables. Toss gently to combine. Taste to adjust the seasonings if necessary. Divide the salad greens among individual plates, top with the pasta salad, and serve.

*Serves 4*

OTHER PASTA CHOICES: ziti or other tubular pasta

# Three-Pepper Pasta Salad

Baked marinated tofu is available in the refrigerated section of natural foods stores. If unavailable, rinsed canned chickpeas or other beans may be added instead. This is a fun salad to adapt for holiday gatherings. For example, at Christmastime, use red and green peppers and add some broccoli florets and cherry tomatoes. For Halloween, use orange and black bell peppers and toss in some grated carrots, black olives, and black beans.

1 pound fusilli
½ cup extra-virgin olive oil
1 green bell pepper
1 red bell pepper
1 yellow bell pepper
8 ounces baked marinated tofu, cut into ½-inch dice
¼ cup red wine vinegar
1 garlic clove, pressed
2 tablespoons minced fresh flat-leaf parsley
Salt and freshly ground black pepper
Salad greens, for serving

Cook the fusilli in a large pot of salted boiling water, stirring occasionally, until it is al dente, about 8 to 10 minutes. When the pasta is cooked, drain it, rinse under cold water, and place in a large serving bowl. Toss with 1 tablespoon of the olive oil and set aside. Halve and seed the bell peppers and place on a baking sheet, skin side up. Place under the broiler until the skins are blackened. Place the peppers in a plastic or paper bag and let stand for about 10 minutes. Remove the charred skin from the peppers and cut into thin strips. Add to the pasta along with the tofu. To make the dressing, combine the vinegar, garlic, parsley, and salt and pepper to taste in a small bowl. Whisk in the remaining olive oil and blend well. Add the dressing to the pasta and toss gently to combine. Serve on top of salad greens on individual plates or in a large shallow serving bowl.

*Serves 4*

OTHER PASTA CHOICES: gemelli, cavatappi

# Ratatouille Radiatore

The flavors of ratatouille, the classic French vegetable mélange, are well suited to pair with pasta. This salad is delicious served at room temperature, making it perfect for a buffet. However, I usually serve it warm for a seated meal. Either way, a crisp salad and warm, crusty bread are good accompaniments.

1 pound radiatore
½ cup extra-virgin olive oil
1 small eggplant, cut into ½-inch dice
2 small zucchini, halved lengthwise and sliced
2 cups thinly sliced mushrooms (about ¾ pound)
Salt and freshly ground black pepper
6 ripe plum tomatoes, coarsely chopped
¼ cup minced fresh flat-leaf parsley
1 tablespoon capers
2 garlic cloves, pressed
3 tablespoons red wine vinegar
2 tablespoons chopped fresh basil leaves

Cook the radiatore in a large pot of salted boiling water, stirring occasionally, until it is al dente, about 8 minutes. When the pasta is cooked, drain it and and rinse under cold water. Place in a large serving bowl, toss with 1 tablespoon of the oil, and set aside. Heat 1 tablespoon of the oil in a skillet over medium heat. Add the eggplant and cook until softened, about 5 minutes. Stir in the zucchini, mushrooms, and salt and pepper to taste, and cook until just softened, about 3 minutes. Stir in the tomatoes, parsley, and capers, and transfer to a bowl. To make the dressing, combine the garlic, vinegar, and salt and pepper to taste in a small bowl. Whisk in the remaining olive oil and pour the dressing over the vegetables. Let the vegetables marinate at room temperature for 30 minutes, then add to the pasta, along with the basil. Taste to adjust the seasonings and serve at room temperature.

*Serves 4*

OTHER PASTA CHOICES: rotini, farfalle

# Artichoke Pasta Salad with Balsamic Vinaigrette

Fresh or frozen artichoke hearts may be used instead of canned. Either gaeta or Kalamata olives would be good choices for this salad, but avoid those canned black olives packed in water—they lack flavor. Serve with warm focaccia for a simple supper.

12 ounces ziti
1 (14-ounce) can artichoke hearts, drained and quartered
3 ripe plum tomatoes, cut into eighths
½ cup black olives, pitted
½ cup extra-virgin olive oil
3 tablespoons balsamic vinegar
Juice and zest of 1 lemon
1 tablespoon minced fresh tarragon, or large pinch dried tarragon, crumbled
Salt and freshly ground black pepper
Salad greens, for serving

Cook the ziti in a large pot of salted boiling water, stirring occasionally, until it is al dente, about 8 to 10 minutes. When the pasta is cooked, drain it, rinse under cold water, and place in a large bowl. Add the artichokes, tomatoes, and olives to the pasta. Toss with 1 tablespoon of the olive oil and set aside. To make the dressing, combine the vinegar, lemon juice and zest, tarragon, remaining oil, and salt and pepper to taste in a small bowl. Blend well and pour over the pasta salad. Toss gently to combine. To serve, divide the salad among individual plates lined with salad greens.

*Serves 4*

OTHER PASTA CHOICES: penne or other tubular pasta

# Lighten Up Macaroni Salad

When I crave the old-fashioned macaroni salad of my youth, I "lighten up" and make it with heart-healthy soy. Serve it alongside grilled tofu hot dogs and veggie burgers for a healthful cookout with all the trimmings.

12 ounces elbow macaroni
½ cup minced celery
1 cup soft or silken tofu
½ cup soy milk or milk
¼ cup grated onion
¼ cup sweet pickle relish
2 tablespoons fresh lemon juice
1 teaspoon Dijon mustard
½ teaspoon salt, or to taste
Cayenne pepper

Cook the macaroni in a large pot of salted boiling water, stirring occasionally, until it is al dente, about 8 minutes. When the pasta is cooked, drain it, rinse under cold water, and place in a large serving bowl. Add the celery and set aside. To make the dressing, in a blender or food processor process the tofu and soy milk until smooth. Add the onion, relish, lemon juice, mustard, salt, and cayenne to taste, and blend well. Add the dressing to the pasta and mix well. Taste to adjust the seasonings. Cover and refrigerate for at least 1 hour before serving.

*Serves 4*

OTHER PASTA CHOICES: small shells, radiatore

# Summer Sunshine Pasta Salad

Evocative of a summer day, seashell and butterfly pastas combine with broccoli florets and sunflower seeds for a whimsical ray of sunshine any time of year. If serving as an entree, add cooked chickpeas or kidney beans to the salad.

8 ounces farfalle
¼ teaspoon turmeric
8 ounces small shells
⅓ cup plus 1 tablespoon extra-virgin olive oil
2 cups broccoli florets, blanched
Juice and zest of 1 orange
2 tablespoons fresh lemon juice
Salt
Cayenne pepper
1 yellow bell pepper, cut into thin strips
1 small red onion, chopped
1 cup cherry tomatoes, halved
¼ cup sunflower seeds

Cook the farfalle in a large pot of salted boiling water, stirring occasionally, until it is al dente, about 8 to 10 minutes. While the farfalle is cooking, add the turmeric to the water to turn the pasta bright yellow. Cook the pasta shells in a separate pot of salted boiling water until they are al dente, about 8 minutes. When both pastas are cooked, drain them and rinse under cold water. Place both pastas in a bowl, toss with 1 tablespoon of the oil, add the broccoli and set aside. To make the dressing, combine the orange juice and zest, lemon juice, and salt and cayenne to taste in a small bowl. Whisk in the remaining oil until blended, then pour dressing over the pasta. Add the bell pepper, onion, and tomatoes, and toss to combine. Sprinkle on the sunflower seeds before serving.

*Serves 4*

OTHER PASTA CHOICES: radiatore, rotini

# Fruity Tropical Pasta Salad

Juicy fresh fruit and creamy coconut milk add a taste of the tropics to this colorful salad. Try it on a warm summer night with grilled jerk-spiced tempeh.

12 ounces small pasta shells
2 cups fresh pineapple chunks
1 mango, peeled, seeded, and cut into ½-inch pieces
1 navel orange, peeled and cut into 1-inch chunks
1 small red bell pepper, cut into thin matchsticks
½ cup minced celery
2 tablespoons minced scallions
2 tablespoons chopped fresh mint
1 cup unsweetened coconut milk
¼ cup fresh orange juice
Juice and zest of 1 lime
1 teaspoon light brown sugar, or to taste
⅛ teaspoon ground allspice
⅛ teaspoon cayenne pepper
Salt
Salad greens, for serving
Toasted shredded coconut

Cook the pasta in a large pot of salted boiling water, stirring occasionally, until it is al dente, about 8 minutes. When the pasta is cooked, drain it, rinse under cold water, and place in a large bowl. Add the pineapple, mango, orange, bell pepper, celery, scallions, and mint, and set aside. To make the dressing, combine the coconut milk, orange juice, lime juice and zest, sugar, allspice, cayenne, and salt to taste in a small bowl, and mix well. Pour the dressing over the pasta salad and toss gently to combine. Serve on a bed of salad greens or in hollowed-out halves of pineapple shells, sprinkled with toasted coconut if you like.

*Serves 4*

OTHER PASTA CHOICES: **rotini, farfalle**

# Cumin-Spiced Pasta Salad with Jalapeño Pesto

Ruote, sometimes called rotelle, is shaped like the small wagon-wheels of the Old West—a fitting choice for this taste of the Southwest.

⅓ cup plus 2 tablespoons extra-virgin olive oil
1 teaspoon ground cumin
12 ounces ruote pasta
1 red onion, chopped
2 or 3 jalapeño chiles, halved and seeded
1 large garlic clove
½ cup cooked pinto beans, drained and rinsed
½ cup coarsely chopped fresh flat-leaf parsley
2 tablespoons lime juice
1 teaspoon brown sugar
½ teaspoon chili powder
Salt
Mixed salad greens, for serving

Heat 2 tablespoons of the oil in a skillet over medium heat. Add the cumin and stir until fragrant, about 30 seconds. Set aside. Cook the pasta in a large pot of salted boiling water, stirring occasionally, until it is al dente, about 8 to 10 minutes. When the pasta is cooked, drain it, rinse under cold water, and place in a bowl. Add the cumin–olive oil mixture and onion, toss to combine, and set aside. In a food processor, pulse the jalapeños and garlic until minced. Add the beans, parsley, lime juice, sugar, chili powder, and salt to taste. With the machine running, pour the remaining oil through the feed tube and process to a smooth paste. Add the pesto to the pasta and toss to coat. To serve, divide the pasta salad among plates lined with salad greens.

*Serves 4*

OTHER PASTA CHOICES: farfalle, penne

# Pinto Bean and Salsa Pasta Toss with Lime and Avocado

With bottled salsa and canned pinto beans, this south-of-the-border salad can be put together in minutes. Serve with warm cornbread and some cold Mexican beer.

12 ounces rotini
1½ cups cooked pinto beans, drained and rinsed
2 cups bottled salsa
2 tablespoons minced fresh cilantro
Salt
2 avocados, peeled, pitted, and cut into ½-inch dice
Juice and zest of 1 lime
2 tablespoons extra-virgin olive oil
Cayenne pepper
Salad greens, for serving

Cook the rotini in a large pot of salted boiling water, stirring occasionally, until it is al dente, about 8 to 10 minutes. When the pasta is cooked, drain it, rinse under cold water, and place in a large bowl. Add the beans, salsa, and cilantro, and toss to combine. Season with salt to taste. To make the dressing, combine the avocados, lime juice and zest, oil, and salt and cayenne to taste in a small bowl. Toss gently to coat the avocados with lime juice. To serve, divide the pasta salad among individual plates lined with salad greens, top with avocado dressing, and serve.

*Serves 4*

OTHER PASTA CHOICES: rotelle, cavatappi

# Spicy Cucumber Pasta Salad

I like to serve this refreshing Asian-inspired salad when I make vegetable sushi, to add substance to the meal. If you like, diced tofu may be added to the salad.

12 ounces linguine

¼ cup plus 1 tablespoon dark sesame oil

2 cucumbers, peeled and halved lengthwise

1 bunch scallions, minced

1 teaspoon Asian chile paste, or to taste

Juice and zest of 2 limes

1 teaspoon sugar

Salt

¼ cup minced fresh cilantro or basil

Cook the linguine in a large pot of salted boiling water, stirring occasionally, until it is al dente, about 8 minutes. When the pasta is cooked, drain it, rinse under cold water, and place in a large serving bowl. Toss with 1 tablespoon of the sesame oil and set aside. Seed the cucumber halves, cut them into ¼-inch slices, and add to the pasta along with the scallions. To make the dressing, combine the remaining sesame oil, chili paste, lime juice and zest, sugar and salt to taste in a small bowl. Pour the dressing over the pasta and cucumbers, sprinkle with cilantro or basil, and toss gently to combine.

*Serves 4*

OTHER PASTA CHOICES: spaghetti, fettuccine

# WINE WITH DINNER?

Just as certain wines are best with different meat and seafood dishes, the same holds true for pasta and other vegetarian dishes. Crisp, dry white wines are best with light vegetable and pasta dishes, or those made with white sauces or olive oil sauces. Strong, spicy sauces or those made with tomatoes or cheese can benefit from the more robust, full flavored red wines.

While wines from other areas of the world can be perfectly suitable to serve with pasta, it can also be fun to pair wine from a particular region with a pasta dish from the same region of Italy. If you are using wine in the sauce, you might complement the flavor by serving the same wine to drink.

Here are some well known Italian wines that complement almost any pasta dish:

- Bardolino—light fruity red from Veneto

- Chianti Classico—rich mellow red from Tuscany

- Pinot Grigio—fruity dry white from Fruili-Venezia

- Soave—light dry white from Veneto

- Valpolicella—robust fruity red from Veneto

# INDEX

The author, at age four with Mom,
perfecting her technique.